50 Food and Drink Recipes for Home

By: Kelly Johnson

Table of Contents

- Spaghetti Carbonara
- Beef Stroganoff
- Chicken Alfredo
- Margherita Pizza
- Chicken Tikka Masala
- Shrimp Scampi
- Greek Salad
- Beef Tacos
- Vegetable Stir-Fry
- Clam Chowder
- Lemon Garlic Salmon
- Chicken Fajitas
- Mushroom Risotto
- Beef Wellington
- Ratatouille
- French Onion Soup
- Pad Thai
- Chicken Parmesan
- Quiche Lorraine
- Baked Ziti
- Fish Tacos
- Caesar Salad
- Stuffed Peppers
- Chicken Pot Pie
- Beef Bourguignon
- Vegetable Curry
- BBQ Ribs
- Lobster Bisque
- Shepherd's Pie
- Shakshuka
- Chicken Marsala
- Eggplant Parmesan
- Paella
- Chicken Cordon Bleu
- Gumbo

- Falafel
- Sushi Rolls
- Beef Chili
- Gazpacho
- Lamb Kebabs
- Pork Schnitzel
- Shrimp Gumbo
- Caprese Salad
- Chicken Satay
- Beef Teriyaki
- Spinach Lasagna
- Peking Duck
- Pork Carnitas
- Moussaka
- Beef Pho

Spaghetti Carbonara

Ingredients:

- 12 oz (340g) spaghetti
- 2 large eggs
- 1 cup grated Pecorino Romano cheese (or Parmesan)
- 4 oz pancetta (or guanciale), diced
- 2 cloves garlic, minced
- Salt and freshly ground black pepper
- Fresh parsley, chopped (optional, for garnish)

Instructions:

1. Cook the Spaghetti:
    - Bring a large pot of salted water to a boil.
    - Add the spaghetti and cook until al dente, according to package instructions.
    - Reserve about 1 cup of pasta water before draining the spaghetti.
2. Prepare the Sauce:
    - In a mixing bowl, whisk together the eggs and grated cheese until well combined.
3. Cook the Pancetta:
    - In a large skillet over medium heat, add the diced pancetta (or guanciale).
    - Cook until it becomes crispy, about 5-7 minutes.
    - Add the minced garlic to the skillet and sauté for an additional minute until fragrant.
4. Combine Spaghetti and Sauce:
    - Add the cooked spaghetti to the skillet with the pancetta and garlic.
    - Remove the skillet from the heat.
    - Pour the egg and cheese mixture over the hot pasta, stirring quickly to create a creamy sauce.
    - If the sauce is too thick, gradually add reserved pasta water, a little at a time, until you reach the desired consistency.
5. Season and Serve:
    - Season with salt and freshly ground black pepper to taste.
    - Garnish with chopped fresh parsley, if desired.
    - Serve immediately with extra grated cheese on the side.

Enjoy your delicious Spaghetti Carbonara!

Beef Stroganoff

Ingredients:

- 1 lb (450g) beef sirloin or tenderloin, thinly sliced
- 2 tablespoons olive oil
- 1 medium onion, finely chopped
- 2 cloves garlic, minced
- 8 oz (225g) mushrooms, sliced
- 1 cup beef broth
- 1 cup sour cream
- 2 tablespoons all-purpose flour
- 2 teaspoons Dijon mustard
- 1 tablespoon Worcestershire sauce
- Salt and freshly ground black pepper
- Fresh parsley, chopped (for garnish)
- Egg noodles or rice, cooked according to package instructions

Instructions:

1. Prepare the Beef:
    - Season the sliced beef with salt and pepper.
    - In a large skillet, heat the olive oil over medium-high heat.
    - Add the beef in batches, cooking until browned on both sides, about 2-3 minutes per side. Remove the beef from the skillet and set aside.
2. Cook the Vegetables:
    - In the same skillet, add the chopped onion and sauté until translucent, about 5 minutes.
    - Add the minced garlic and sliced mushrooms, cooking until the mushrooms are tender and the liquid has evaporated, about 5-7 minutes.
3. Make the Sauce:
    - Sprinkle the flour over the mushroom mixture and stir well to combine.
    - Gradually pour in the beef broth, stirring constantly to avoid lumps.
    - Bring the mixture to a simmer and cook until it thickens slightly, about 5 minutes.
    - Stir in the sour cream, Dijon mustard, and Worcestershire sauce until well combined.
4. Combine and Serve:
    - Return the browned beef to the skillet and stir to coat with the sauce.

- Cook for an additional 2-3 minutes, or until the beef is heated through.
- Taste and adjust seasoning with salt and pepper as needed.
- Serve the beef stroganoff over cooked egg noodles or rice.
- Garnish with chopped fresh parsley.

Enjoy your Beef Stroganoff!

Chicken Alfredo

Ingredients:

- 2 boneless, skinless chicken breasts
- Salt and freshly ground black pepper
- 2 tablespoons olive oil
- 12 oz (340g) fettuccine pasta
- 1 cup heavy cream
- 1 cup grated Parmesan cheese
- 4 tablespoons unsalted butter
- 3 cloves garlic, minced
- Fresh parsley, chopped (optional, for garnish)

Instructions:

1. Cook the Fettuccine:
    - Bring a large pot of salted water to a boil.
    - Add the fettuccine and cook until al dente, according to package instructions.
    - Reserve about 1 cup of pasta water before draining the pasta.
2. Prepare the Chicken:
    - Season both sides of the chicken breasts with salt and pepper.
    - In a large skillet, heat the olive oil over medium-high heat.
    - Add the chicken breasts and cook until golden brown and cooked through, about 5-7 minutes per side.
    - Remove the chicken from the skillet and let it rest for a few minutes before slicing into thin strips.
3. Make the Alfredo Sauce:
    - In the same skillet, reduce the heat to medium.
    - Add the butter and let it melt.
    - Add the minced garlic and sauté until fragrant, about 1 minute.
    - Pour in the heavy cream and bring it to a gentle simmer.
    - Gradually whisk in the grated Parmesan cheese until the sauce is smooth and creamy.
    - If the sauce is too thick, add a bit of the reserved pasta water until you reach the desired consistency.
4. Combine and Serve:

- Add the cooked fettuccine to the skillet with the Alfredo sauce, tossing to coat the pasta evenly.
- Add the sliced chicken on top and gently mix to combine.
- Taste and adjust seasoning with salt and pepper if needed.
- Garnish with chopped fresh parsley if desired.

Enjoy your Chicken Alfredo!

Margherita Pizza

Ingredients:

- 1 pizza dough ball (store-bought or homemade)
- 1/2 cup pizza sauce (store-bought or homemade)
- 8 oz (225g) fresh mozzarella cheese, sliced
- 2-3 medium tomatoes, thinly sliced
- Fresh basil leaves
- 2 tablespoons extra-virgin olive oil
- Salt and freshly ground black pepper
- Cornmeal (for dusting)

Instructions:

1. Preheat the Oven:
    - Preheat your oven to 475°F (245°C) with a pizza stone or baking sheet inside.
2. Prepare the Dough:
    - On a lightly floured surface, roll out the pizza dough to your desired thickness (about 12 inches in diameter for a medium pizza).
    - Transfer the dough to a piece of parchment paper dusted with cornmeal to prevent sticking.
3. Assemble the Pizza:
    - Spread the pizza sauce evenly over the dough, leaving a small border for the crust.
    - Arrange the fresh mozzarella slices evenly over the sauce.
    - Lay the tomato slices on top of the cheese.
    - Tear a few fresh basil leaves and sprinkle them over the pizza.
4. Bake the Pizza:
    - Carefully transfer the assembled pizza (with the parchment paper) onto the preheated pizza stone or baking sheet.
    - Bake for 10-12 minutes, or until the crust is golden brown and the cheese is melted and bubbly.
5. Finish and Serve:
    - Remove the pizza from the oven and drizzle with extra-virgin olive oil.
    - Season with salt and freshly ground black pepper to taste.
    - Garnish with additional fresh basil leaves.
    - Let the pizza cool for a few minutes before slicing and serving.

Enjoy your Margherita Pizza!

Chicken Tikka Masala

Ingredients:

For the Chicken Marinade:

- 1 lb (450g) boneless, skinless chicken breasts, cut into bite-sized pieces
- 1 cup plain yogurt
- 2 tablespoons lemon juice
- 2 teaspoons ground cumin
- 2 teaspoons ground coriander
- 1 teaspoon ground turmeric
- 1 teaspoon ground paprika
- 1 teaspoon ground garam masala
- 1 teaspoon ground black pepper
- 1 teaspoon salt
- 2 cloves garlic, minced
- 1-inch piece ginger, grated

For the Sauce:

- 2 tablespoons vegetable oil or ghee
- 1 large onion, finely chopped
- 2 cloves garlic, minced
- 1-inch piece ginger, grated
- 1-2 green chilies, chopped (optional)
- 1 tablespoon ground cumin
- 1 tablespoon ground coriander
- 1 teaspoon ground turmeric
- 1 teaspoon ground paprika
- 1 teaspoon ground garam masala
- 1 teaspoon ground cayenne pepper (optional, for extra heat)
- 1 (14 oz) can tomato puree
- 1 cup heavy cream
- Salt and freshly ground black pepper to taste
- Fresh cilantro, chopped (for garnish)

Instructions:

1. Marinate the Chicken:
   - In a large bowl, combine all the marinade ingredients.
   - Add the chicken pieces and mix well to coat.
   - Cover and refrigerate for at least 1 hour, or overnight for best results.
2. Cook the Chicken:
   - Preheat your grill or broiler to high heat.
   - Thread the marinated chicken pieces onto skewers.
   - Grill or broil the chicken for about 5-7 minutes on each side, or until cooked through and slightly charred. Remove from skewers and set aside.
3. Make the Sauce:
   - In a large skillet or saucepan, heat the vegetable oil or ghee over medium heat.
   - Add the chopped onion and sauté until golden brown, about 5-7 minutes.
   - Add the minced garlic, grated ginger, and chopped green chilies (if using), and sauté for another 2 minutes.
   - Add the ground cumin, ground coriander, ground turmeric, ground paprika, ground garam masala, and ground cayenne pepper (if using). Stir well to combine and cook for 1-2 minutes until fragrant.
   - Stir in the tomato puree and bring the mixture to a simmer. Cook for about 10 minutes, stirring occasionally, until the sauce thickens.
   - Reduce the heat to low and stir in the heavy cream. Simmer for another 5 minutes, stirring occasionally. Adjust seasoning with salt and black pepper to taste.
4. Combine and Serve:
   - Add the grilled chicken pieces to the sauce and stir well to coat.
   - Simmer for an additional 5-10 minutes to let the flavors meld together.
   - Garnish with chopped fresh cilantro.

Serve your Chicken Tikka Masala with steamed basmati rice or warm naan bread. Enjoy!

Shrimp Scampi

Ingredients:

- 1 lb (450g) large shrimp, peeled and deveined
- Salt and freshly ground black pepper
- 3 tablespoons olive oil
- 4 tablespoons unsalted butter
- 4 cloves garlic, minced
- 1/2 teaspoon red pepper flakes (optional)
- 1/2 cup dry white wine or chicken broth
- 1 lemon, juiced
- 1/4 cup fresh parsley, chopped
- 12 oz (340g) linguine or spaghetti
- Grated Parmesan cheese (optional, for serving)

Instructions:

1. Cook the Pasta:
    - Bring a large pot of salted water to a boil.
    - Add the linguine or spaghetti and cook until al dente, according to package instructions.
    - Reserve about 1/2 cup of pasta water before draining the pasta.
2. Prepare the Shrimp:
    - Pat the shrimp dry with paper towels and season with salt and pepper.
3. Cook the Shrimp:
    - In a large skillet, heat 2 tablespoons of olive oil over medium-high heat.
    - Add the shrimp in a single layer and cook for 2-3 minutes per side, until pink and opaque. Remove the shrimp from the skillet and set aside.
4. Make the Sauce:
    - In the same skillet, lower the heat to medium and add the butter.
    - Once the butter has melted, add the minced garlic and red pepper flakes (if using). Sauté for about 1 minute until the garlic is fragrant but not browned.
    - Pour in the white wine (or chicken broth) and bring to a simmer. Cook for about 2-3 minutes, or until the liquid is reduced by half.
    - Stir in the lemon juice and season with salt and pepper to taste.
5. Combine and Serve:
    - Return the cooked shrimp to the skillet and toss to coat in the sauce.

- Add the cooked pasta to the skillet and toss to combine, adding reserved pasta water a little at a time until the sauce reaches your desired consistency.
- Stir in the chopped fresh parsley.
- Serve immediately, with grated Parmesan cheese on the side if desired.

Enjoy your Shrimp Scampi!

Greek Salad

Ingredients:

- 4 cups ripe tomatoes, cut into wedges or large chunks
- 1 cucumber, sliced into half-moons
- 1 red onion, thinly sliced
- 1 green bell pepper, sliced into rings
- 1/2 cup Kalamata olives
- 8 oz (225g) feta cheese, cut into blocks
- 1/4 cup extra-virgin olive oil
- 2 tablespoons red wine vinegar
- 1 teaspoon dried oregano
- Salt and freshly ground black pepper to taste
- Fresh oregano or parsley for garnish (optional)

Instructions:

1. Prepare the Vegetables:
   - In a large salad bowl, combine the tomatoes, cucumber, red onion, green bell pepper, and Kalamata olives.
2. Add the Feta:
   - Place the blocks of feta cheese on top of the salad.
3. Make the Dressing:
   - In a small bowl or jar, whisk together the extra-virgin olive oil, red wine vinegar, dried oregano, salt, and freshly ground black pepper.
4. Dress the Salad:
   - Pour the dressing over the salad.
   - Toss gently to combine, being careful not to break up the feta too much.
5. Garnish and Serve:
   - Garnish with fresh oregano or parsley if desired.
   - Serve immediately.

Enjoy your Greek Salad!

Beef Tacos

Ingredients:

- 1 pound (450g) ground beef
- 1 small onion, diced
- 2 cloves garlic, minced
- 1 tablespoon chili powder
- 1 teaspoon ground cumin
- 1/2 teaspoon paprika
- 1/4 teaspoon dried oregano
- Salt and pepper to taste
- 1/4 cup (60ml) beef broth or water
- 8 small tortillas (corn or flour)
- Toppings: shredded lettuce, diced tomatoes, shredded cheese, salsa, sour cream, avocado slices, etc.

Instructions:

1. Cook the Beef Filling:
    - Heat a skillet over medium heat. Add the ground beef and cook until browned, breaking it apart with a spoon as it cooks.
    - Add the diced onion and minced garlic to the skillet with the beef. Cook until the onion is translucent and the garlic is fragrant, about 2-3 minutes.
    - Stir in the chili powder, ground cumin, paprika, dried oregano, salt, and pepper. Cook for another minute to toast the spices.
    - Pour in the beef broth or water and simmer for a few minutes until the liquid has reduced and the beef is coated in a flavorful sauce. Remove from heat.
2. Warm the Tortillas:
    - If using corn tortillas, warm them in a dry skillet over medium heat for about 30 seconds on each side, or until soft and pliable. If using flour tortillas, you can warm them in the microwave or in a skillet for a few seconds on each side.
3. Assemble the Tacos:
    - Spoon a portion of the beef filling onto each tortilla.
    - Add your favorite toppings such as shredded lettuce, diced tomatoes, shredded cheese, salsa, sour cream, and avocado slices.
4. Serve:

- Serve the beef tacos immediately, and enjoy!

Feel free to customize your beef tacos with additional toppings or adjust the seasonings to suit your taste preferences. Enjoy your homemade beef tacos!

Vegetable Stir-Fry

Ingredients:

- Assorted vegetables (e.g., bell peppers, broccoli, carrots, snap peas, mushrooms, onions, zucchini, etc.), sliced or chopped
- 2 tablespoons vegetable oil (or any cooking oil with a high smoke point)
- 2 cloves garlic, minced
- 1-inch piece of ginger, minced or grated
- Soy sauce or tamari, to taste
- Salt and pepper, to taste
- Optional: sliced tofu, chicken, beef, or shrimp for added protein
- Optional toppings: sesame seeds, chopped green onions, cilantro, etc.

Instructions:

1. Prepare the Vegetables:
    - Wash and chop your choice of vegetables into bite-sized pieces. Ensure they are uniform in size for even cooking.
2. Heat the Oil:
    - Heat the vegetable oil in a large skillet or wok over medium-high heat.
3. Add Aromatics:
    - Add the minced garlic and ginger to the hot oil. Stir-fry for about 30 seconds until fragrant, being careful not to burn them.
4. Stir-Fry the Vegetables:
    - Add the sliced vegetables to the skillet. Stir-fry continuously for 4-5 minutes or until they are crisp-tender. You want them to retain some of their crunch.
5. Seasoning:
    - Season the stir-fry with soy sauce or tamari to taste. Be mindful not to add too much salt if your soy sauce is already salty. Add salt and pepper if needed.
6. Optional Protein:
    - If using tofu, chicken, beef, or shrimp, add it to the skillet along with the vegetables and cook until heated through or until the protein is cooked to your liking.
7. Final Touches:
    - Taste and adjust the seasoning if necessary.

- If desired, sprinkle sesame seeds, chopped green onions, or cilantro on top for garnish.
8. Serve:
    - Serve the vegetable stir-fry hot as is, or over cooked rice or noodles.

Feel free to experiment with different vegetable combinations and seasonings to create your perfect vegetable stir-fry. It's a versatile and healthy dish that's great for any occasion. Enjoy your homemade vegetable stir-fry!

Clam Chowder

Ingredients:

- 6 slices bacon, chopped
- 1 medium onion, finely chopped
- 2 celery stalks, finely chopped
- 3 cloves garlic, minced
- 3 tablespoons all-purpose flour
- 3 cups clam juice (from canned clams) or fish stock
- 2 cups whole milk
- 2 cups half-and-half (or heavy cream for a richer chowder)
- 1 bay leaf
- 1 pound (about 450g) russet potatoes, peeled and diced into small cubes
- 2 (6.5-ounce) cans chopped clams, drained, juice reserved
- Salt and black pepper to taste
- Chopped fresh parsley or chives for garnish (optional)

Instructions:

1. Cook Bacon:
    - In a large pot or Dutch oven, cook the chopped bacon over medium heat until crispy. Remove the bacon with a slotted spoon and set aside on a paper towel-lined plate. Leave the bacon fat in the pot.
2. Sauté Vegetables:
    - In the same pot with the bacon fat, add the chopped onion, celery, and minced garlic. Sauté for about 5 minutes, or until the vegetables are softened.
3. Make Roux:
    - Sprinkle the flour over the sautéed vegetables and stir to coat. Cook for an additional 2 minutes to cook out the raw flour taste.
4. Add Liquids:
    - Gradually pour in the clam juice (or fish stock), whole milk, and half-and-half while stirring constantly to avoid lumps. Add the bay leaf. Bring the mixture to a simmer.
5. Add Potatoes:
    - Add the diced potatoes to the pot. Simmer for about 15-20 minutes, or until the potatoes are tender.
6. Add Clams:

- Add the drained chopped clams to the pot. Stir in the reserved clam juice. Simmer for an additional 5 minutes.
7. Season and Serve:
    - Season the clam chowder with salt and black pepper to taste. Remove the bay leaf. Stir in the crispy bacon. Taste and adjust seasoning if necessary.
    - Ladle the clam chowder into bowls and garnish with chopped fresh parsley or chives if desired.
    - Serve hot with crusty bread or oyster crackers.

Enjoy your homemade New England clam chowder! It's rich, creamy, and full of comforting flavors.

Lemon Garlic Salmon

Ingredients:

- 4 salmon fillets (about 6 ounces each), skin-on or skinless
- 2 tablespoons olive oil
- 4 cloves garlic, minced
- Zest of 1 lemon
- Juice of 1 lemon
- 2 tablespoons chopped fresh parsley
- Salt and black pepper to taste
- Lemon slices for garnish (optional)

Instructions:

1. Preheat Oven:
    - Preheat your oven to 400°F (200°C). Line a baking sheet with parchment paper or foil for easy cleanup.
2. Prepare Salmon:
    - Pat the salmon fillets dry with paper towels. Season both sides of the salmon with salt and black pepper to taste.
3. Make Lemon Garlic Mixture:
    - In a small bowl, combine the minced garlic, lemon zest, lemon juice, chopped parsley, and olive oil.
4. Coat Salmon:
    - Place the salmon fillets on the prepared baking sheet. Spoon the lemon garlic mixture evenly over the top of each fillet, spreading it out to cover the surface.
5. Bake Salmon:
    - Bake the salmon in the preheated oven for about 12-15 minutes, or until the salmon is cooked through and flakes easily with a fork. Cooking time may vary depending on the thickness of your salmon fillets.
6. Broil (Optional):
    - For an extra golden crust on top, you can broil the salmon for 1-2 minutes after baking. Keep a close eye on it to prevent burning.
7. Serve:
    - Once cooked, remove the salmon from the oven. Garnish with lemon slices if desired.

- Serve the lemon garlic salmon hot with your favorite side dishes, such as roasted vegetables, rice, or salad.

This lemon garlic salmon is bursting with flavor and pairs wonderfully with the bright citrus and herb notes. It's perfect for a quick weeknight dinner or a special occasion meal. Enjoy!

Chicken Fajitas

Ingredients:

- 1 pound (about 450g) boneless, skinless chicken breasts, thinly sliced
- 2 bell peppers (any color), thinly sliced
- 1 onion, thinly sliced
- 2 cloves garlic, minced
- 2 tablespoons vegetable oil
- 2 tablespoons fajita seasoning mix (store-bought or homemade*)
- Salt and black pepper to taste
- 8 small flour tortillas
- Optional toppings: shredded cheese, sour cream, guacamole, salsa, chopped cilantro, lime wedges, etc.

Instructions:

1. Marinate the Chicken (optional):
    - If time allows, marinate the sliced chicken breasts in some of the fajita seasoning mix and a tablespoon of vegetable oil for about 30 minutes to enhance the flavor.
2. Prepare Vegetables:
    - Heat one tablespoon of vegetable oil in a large skillet over medium-high heat. Add the sliced bell peppers and onion to the skillet. Cook, stirring occasionally, until they are softened and slightly caramelized, about 5-7 minutes. Remove the vegetables from the skillet and set aside.
3. Cook Chicken:
    - In the same skillet, add another tablespoon of vegetable oil if needed. Add the sliced chicken breasts to the skillet. Season with salt, black pepper, and the remaining fajita seasoning mix. Cook, stirring occasionally, until the chicken is cooked through and no longer pink, about 6-8 minutes.
4. Combine Ingredients:
    - Return the cooked vegetables to the skillet with the chicken. Add minced garlic and toss everything together. Cook for an additional 1-2 minutes to allow the flavors to meld.
5. Warm Tortillas:
    - Meanwhile, warm the flour tortillas in a dry skillet or microwave according to the package instructions.
6. Assemble Fajitas:

- Spoon the chicken and vegetable mixture onto the warm tortillas.
7. Add Toppings:
    - Serve the chicken fajitas with your favorite toppings such as shredded cheese, sour cream, guacamole, salsa, chopped cilantro, and lime wedges.
8. Serve:
    - Roll up the tortillas and serve the chicken fajitas immediately while warm.

Enjoy your homemade chicken fajitas with all the delicious toppings and flavors! They make for a fun and customizable meal that's perfect for gatherings or busy weeknights.

*For homemade fajita seasoning mix, you can combine ingredients like chili powder, cumin, paprika, garlic powder, onion powder, oregano, salt, and black pepper to taste. Adjust the spices according to your preference.

Mushroom Risotto

Ingredients:

- 1 1/2 cups Arborio rice
- 6 cups vegetable or chicken broth
- 1/2 cup dry white wine
- 2 tablespoons olive oil
- 2 tablespoons unsalted butter
- 1 onion, finely chopped
- 2 cloves garlic, minced
- 10 ounces (about 300g) mushrooms (such as cremini, shiitake, or button mushrooms), sliced
- 1/2 cup grated Parmesan cheese
- Salt and black pepper to taste
- Fresh parsley, chopped, for garnish (optional)

Instructions:

1. Prepare Broth:
   - In a saucepan, heat the vegetable or chicken broth over medium heat until warm. Keep it warm on low heat throughout the cooking process.
2. Sauté Mushrooms:
   - In a large skillet or Dutch oven, heat 1 tablespoon of olive oil and 1 tablespoon of butter over medium heat. Add the sliced mushrooms and sauté until they are golden brown and tender, about 5-7 minutes. Season with salt and black pepper to taste. Remove the mushrooms from the skillet and set aside.
3. Sauté Onion and Garlic:
   - In the same skillet, add the remaining tablespoon of olive oil and tablespoon of butter. Add the finely chopped onion and minced garlic. Sauté until the onion is translucent and the garlic is fragrant, about 2-3 minutes.
4. Toast Rice:
   - Add the Arborio rice to the skillet with the onion and garlic. Stir well to coat the rice with the oil and butter. Cook for 1-2 minutes, stirring frequently, until the rice is lightly toasted.
5. Deglaze with Wine:

- Pour in the dry white wine and stir continuously until the wine is absorbed by the rice.
6. Add Broth:
    - Begin adding the warm broth to the skillet, one ladleful at a time, stirring frequently. Allow the rice to absorb the broth before adding more. Continue this process until the rice is cooked al dente and has a creamy consistency, about 18-20 minutes. You may not need to use all the broth.
7. Incorporate Mushrooms:
    - Once the risotto is cooked to your desired consistency, stir in the sautéed mushrooms and grated Parmesan cheese. Taste and adjust seasoning with salt and black pepper if needed.
8. Serve:
    - Garnish the mushroom risotto with chopped fresh parsley if desired. Serve hot, and enjoy!

Mushroom risotto is best served immediately while it's still creamy and hot. It's a classic Italian dish that's sure to impress your family and friends. Buon appetito!

Beef Wellington

Ingredients:

- 1 1/2 pounds (about 680g) beef tenderloin or fillet
- Salt and black pepper to taste
- 2 tablespoons olive oil
- 1 tablespoon Dijon mustard
- 1 tablespoon butter
- 8 ounces (about 225g) mushrooms, finely chopped
- 2 cloves garlic, minced
- 1 small onion, finely chopped
- 2 tablespoons chopped fresh parsley
- 1 sheet puff pastry, thawed if frozen
- 4 slices prosciutto or Parma ham
- 1 egg, beaten (for egg wash)
- Optional: beef or mushroom sauce for serving

Instructions:

1. Preheat Oven:
   - Preheat your oven to 400°F (200°C).
2. Prepare Beef:
   - Season the beef fillet generously with salt and black pepper. Heat olive oil in a skillet over high heat. Sear the beef on all sides until browned, about 2 minutes per side. Remove from heat and let it cool slightly.
3. Brush with Mustard:
   - Brush the seared beef fillet with Dijon mustard. This adds flavor and helps the puff pastry adhere.
4. Prepare Mushroom Duxelles:
   - In the same skillet, melt butter over medium heat. Add finely chopped mushrooms, minced garlic, and chopped onion. Cook until the mushrooms release their moisture and the mixture becomes dry, about 8-10 minutes. Stir in chopped parsley. Let the mushroom duxelles mixture cool.
5. Assemble Beef Wellington:
   - Lay out a sheet of plastic wrap on a clean surface. Arrange the slices of prosciutto or Parma ham on the plastic wrap, slightly overlapping. Spread the cooled mushroom duxelles mixture evenly over the ham.
   - Place the seared beef fillet on top of the mushroom mixture.

- Using the plastic wrap to help, tightly roll the ham and mushroom mixture around the beef fillet to form a log shape. Chill in the refrigerator for 15-20 minutes to firm up.

6. Wrap in Puff Pastry:
   - Roll out the puff pastry on a lightly floured surface to a size large enough to wrap the beef completely. Place the chilled beef log in the center of the pastry and wrap it tightly, sealing the edges.
   - Trim any excess pastry and seal the edges by pressing with a fork. Score the top of the pastry lightly with a sharp knife for decoration.

7. Bake:
   - Transfer the wrapped Beef Wellington to a baking sheet lined with parchment paper. Brush the pastry with beaten egg for a golden finish.
   - Bake in the preheated oven for 25-30 minutes, or until the pastry is golden brown and the beef reaches your desired level of doneness (medium-rare is recommended for tenderloin).

8. Rest and Serve:
   - Allow the Beef Wellington to rest for 10 minutes before slicing. This helps the juices redistribute.
   - Slice into thick portions and serve with your favorite sauce, such as beef or mushroom sauce.

Beef Wellington is a show-stopping dish perfect for special occasions. Enjoy the rich flavors and elegant presentation of this classic recipe!

Ratatouille

Ingredients:

- 1 large eggplant, diced
- 2 medium zucchini, diced
- 1 large onion, diced
- 1 red bell pepper, diced
- 1 yellow bell pepper, diced
- 3 cloves garlic, minced
- 4 large tomatoes, diced (or 1 can of diced tomatoes)
- 2 tablespoons tomato paste
- 2 tablespoons olive oil
- 1 teaspoon dried thyme
- 1 teaspoon dried oregano
- Salt and black pepper to taste
- Fresh basil leaves, chopped, for garnish

Instructions:

1. Prepare the Vegetables:
    - Wash and dice all the vegetables into uniform pieces.
2. Sauté Onion and Garlic:
    - Heat olive oil in a large skillet or Dutch oven over medium heat. Add the diced onion and minced garlic. Sauté until the onion is translucent and the garlic is fragrant, about 3-4 minutes.
3. Add Bell Peppers and Eggplant:
    - Add the diced red and yellow bell peppers, as well as the diced eggplant, to the skillet. Cook for another 5 minutes, stirring occasionally, until the vegetables start to soften.
4. Add Zucchini and Tomatoes:
    - Add the diced zucchini and diced tomatoes (or canned tomatoes with their juices) to the skillet. Stir in the tomato paste, dried thyme, dried oregano, salt, and black pepper. Mix well to combine.
5. Simmer:
    - Reduce the heat to low and let the ratatouille simmer gently for about 20-25 minutes, stirring occasionally, until all the vegetables are tender and the flavors have melded together. If the mixture becomes too dry, you can add a splash of water or vegetable broth.

6. Adjust Seasoning:
    - Taste the ratatouille and adjust the seasoning with salt and pepper if needed.
7. Serve:
    - Once the ratatouille is cooked to your liking, remove it from the heat. Garnish with chopped fresh basil leaves just before serving.
    - Ratatouille can be served hot, warm, or at room temperature. It's delicious on its own as a vegetarian main dish or served as a side dish alongside grilled meats or fish.
8. Store:
    - Leftover ratatouille can be stored in an airtight container in the refrigerator for up to 3-4 days. It also freezes well for longer storage.

Enjoy your homemade ratatouille, a flavorful and nutritious dish that celebrates the beauty of seasonal vegetables!

French Onion Soup

Ingredients:

- 4 large onions, thinly sliced
- 2 tablespoons butter
- 2 tablespoons olive oil
- 2 cloves garlic, minced
- 1 teaspoon granulated sugar (optional, to aid caramelization)
- 1/2 cup dry white wine (optional)
- 6 cups beef broth (or vegetable broth for a vegetarian version)
- 1 bay leaf
- Salt and black pepper to taste
- Baguette slices, toasted
- Gruyère cheese, grated (or Swiss cheese)
- Fresh thyme or parsley for garnish (optional)

Instructions:

1. Caramelize Onions:
    - In a large pot or Dutch oven, melt the butter and olive oil over medium heat. Add the thinly sliced onions and cook, stirring occasionally, until they are soft and caramelized, about 30-40 minutes. If desired, sprinkle sugar over the onions to aid caramelization.
2. Add Garlic:
    - Stir in the minced garlic and cook for an additional 1-2 minutes until fragrant.
3. Deglaze with Wine (optional):
    - Pour in the dry white wine to deglaze the pot, scraping up any browned bits from the bottom. Allow the wine to simmer for a few minutes to reduce slightly.
4. Add Broth and Seasonings:
    - Pour in the beef broth and add the bay leaf. Season with salt and black pepper to taste. Bring the soup to a simmer and let it cook for about 20-30 minutes to allow the flavors to meld together.
5. Toast Baguette Slices:
    - While the soup is simmering, preheat the oven broiler. Arrange baguette slices on a baking sheet and toast them under the broiler until golden brown on both sides.

6. Assemble Soup Bowls:
    - Once the soup is ready, discard the bay leaf. Ladle the hot soup into oven-safe bowls. Place a couple of toasted baguette slices on top of each bowl.
7. Add Cheese:
    - Sprinkle grated Gruyère cheese (or Swiss cheese) generously over the baguette slices and the surface of the soup.
8. Broil:
    - Place the soup bowls under the broiler and broil until the cheese is melted, bubbly, and lightly browned on top, about 2-3 minutes. Keep a close eye on them to prevent burning.
9. Serve:
    - Carefully remove the soup bowls from the oven. Garnish with fresh thyme or parsley if desired. Serve hot and enjoy immediately.

French onion soup is best served piping hot, straight from the oven. It's a comforting and satisfying dish perfect for chilly days or as an elegant starter for a special meal.

Pad Thai

Ingredients:

For the Pad Thai Sauce:

- 3 tablespoons tamarind paste
- 3 tablespoons fish sauce
- 2 tablespoons soy sauce
- 2 tablespoons brown sugar (or palm sugar)
- 1 tablespoon rice vinegar
- 1/2 teaspoon chili flakes (adjust to taste)
- 1/4 cup water

For the Pad Thai:

- 8 ounces (about 225g) rice noodles (preferably flat, medium-width)
- 2 tablespoons vegetable oil
- 2 cloves garlic, minced
- 1 small onion, thinly sliced
- 2 eggs, lightly beaten
- 8 ounces (about 225g) protein of your choice (shrimp, chicken, tofu, or a combination)
- 1 cup bean sprouts
- 1 cup shredded carrots
- 4 green onions, sliced
- 1/4 cup chopped peanuts
- Lime wedges for serving
- Fresh cilantro for garnish (optional)

Instructions:

1. Prepare Rice Noodles:
    - Soak the rice noodles in warm water for about 30 minutes, or according to package instructions, until they are softened. Drain and set aside.
2. Make Pad Thai Sauce:
    - In a small bowl, whisk together the tamarind paste, fish sauce, soy sauce, brown sugar, rice vinegar, chili flakes, and water until well combined. Set aside.

3. Cook Protein:
   - Heat 1 tablespoon of vegetable oil in a large skillet or wok over medium-high heat. Add the minced garlic and sliced onion. Stir-fry for about 1-2 minutes until fragrant.
   - Add the protein of your choice (shrimp, chicken, tofu, etc.) to the skillet. Cook until the protein is cooked through. If using shrimp, they should turn pink and opaque. Remove the cooked protein from the skillet and set aside.
4. Stir-Fry Vegetables:
   - In the same skillet, add the remaining tablespoon of vegetable oil. Add the beaten eggs and scramble until just set. Add the soaked rice noodles to the skillet along with the bean sprouts, shredded carrots, and green onions. Stir-fry for 2-3 minutes until the vegetables are slightly softened.
5. Add Sauce and Protein:
   - Pour the prepared Pad Thai sauce over the noodles and vegetables in the skillet. Toss everything together until well coated with the sauce.
   - Return the cooked protein to the skillet and toss to combine with the noodles and vegetables. Cook for an additional 1-2 minutes to heat through.
6. Serve:
   - Transfer the Pad Thai to serving plates or bowls. Garnish with chopped peanuts and fresh cilantro (if using). Serve with lime wedges on the side for squeezing over the Pad Thai just before eating.

Enjoy your homemade Pad Thai, a flavorful and satisfying Thai noodle dish that's perfect for any occasion! Adjust the ingredients and seasonings according to your taste preferences.

Chicken Parmesan

Ingredients:

For the Chicken:

- 4 boneless, skinless chicken breasts
- Salt and black pepper to taste
- 1 cup all-purpose flour
- 2 large eggs, beaten
- 1 cup breadcrumbs (plain or seasoned)
- 1/2 cup grated Parmesan cheese
- Vegetable oil for frying

For Assembly:

- 2 cups marinara sauce (homemade or store-bought)
- 1 cup shredded mozzarella cheese
- 1/4 cup grated Parmesan cheese
- Fresh basil leaves for garnish (optional)
- Cooked spaghetti or pasta for serving (optional)

Instructions:

1. Prepare Chicken:
   - Preheat the oven to 375°F (190°C). Season the chicken breasts with salt and black pepper on both sides.
2. Coat Chicken:
   - Set up a breading station with three shallow bowls. Place the flour in one bowl, beaten eggs in another bowl, and a mixture of breadcrumbs and grated Parmesan cheese in the third bowl.
   - Dredge each chicken breast in the flour, shaking off any excess. Dip it into the beaten eggs, allowing any excess to drip off. Finally, coat the chicken in the breadcrumb-Parmesan mixture, pressing gently to adhere.
3. Fry Chicken:
   - In a large skillet, heat vegetable oil over medium-high heat. Carefully place the breaded chicken breasts in the hot oil and cook until golden brown and crispy on both sides, about 3-4 minutes per side. You may need to work in

batches to avoid overcrowding the skillet. Transfer the fried chicken to a paper towel-lined plate to drain excess oil.
4. Assemble Chicken Parmesan:
    - Spread a thin layer of marinara sauce on the bottom of a baking dish. Place the fried chicken breasts in the baking dish in a single layer.
    - Spoon additional marinara sauce over each chicken breast, covering them completely.
    - Sprinkle shredded mozzarella cheese and grated Parmesan cheese over the top of each chicken breast, ensuring they are evenly coated.
5. Bake:
    - Transfer the baking dish to the preheated oven and bake for 20-25 minutes, or until the cheese is melted and bubbly, and the chicken is cooked through with an internal temperature of 165°F (75°C).
6. Serve:
    - Once cooked, remove the Chicken Parmesan from the oven. Garnish with fresh basil leaves if desired. Serve hot, accompanied by cooked spaghetti or pasta if desired.

Enjoy your homemade Chicken Parmesan, a delicious and comforting Italian-American classic that's sure to please your family and friends!

Quiche Lorraine

Ingredients:

For the Crust:

- 1 1/4 cups all-purpose flour
- 1/2 teaspoon salt
- 1/2 cup (1 stick) unsalted butter, cold and diced
- 3-4 tablespoons ice water

For the Filling:

- 6 slices bacon, chopped
- 1 small onion, finely chopped
- 1 cup shredded Swiss cheese (Gruyère or Emmental)
- 4 large eggs
- 1 cup heavy cream (or half-and-half)
- 1/2 teaspoon salt
- 1/4 teaspoon black pepper
- Pinch of ground nutmeg

Instructions:

1. Prepare Crust:
   - In a food processor, pulse the flour and salt until combined. Add the diced cold butter and pulse until the mixture resembles coarse crumbs.
   - Gradually add the ice water, 1 tablespoon at a time, pulsing until the dough comes together and forms a ball. Be careful not to overwork the dough.
   - Flatten the dough into a disk, wrap it in plastic wrap, and refrigerate for at least 30 minutes.
2. Preheat Oven:
   - Preheat your oven to 375°F (190°C).
3. Roll Out Crust:
   - On a lightly floured surface, roll out the chilled dough into a circle slightly larger than your tart pan. Carefully transfer the dough to a 9-inch tart pan with a removable bottom. Press the dough into the bottom and sides of the pan. Trim any excess dough.
4. Par-Bake Crust:

- Line the crust with parchment paper and fill it with pie weights or dried beans. Bake in the preheated oven for about 15 minutes. Remove the parchment paper and weights, and continue baking for another 5 minutes until the crust is lightly golden. Remove from the oven and let it cool slightly.

5. Prepare Filling:
   - In a skillet, cook the chopped bacon over medium heat until crispy. Remove the bacon from the skillet and place it on a paper towel-lined plate to drain excess grease. In the same skillet, sauté the chopped onion until softened. Remove from heat and let it cool slightly.

6. Assemble Quiche:
   - Sprinkle the cooked bacon and sautéed onion evenly over the par-baked crust. Sprinkle shredded Swiss cheese on top.

7. Make Custard Filling:
   - In a mixing bowl, whisk together the eggs, heavy cream, salt, black pepper, and ground nutmeg until well combined.

8. Bake Quiche:
   - Pour the custard filling over the bacon, onion, and cheese in the tart shell.
   - Place the quiche in the preheated oven and bake for 30-35 minutes, or until the custard is set and the top is golden brown.

9. Serve:
   - Once baked, remove the Quiche Lorraine from the oven and let it cool for a few minutes before slicing. Serve warm or at room temperature.

Enjoy your homemade Quiche Lorraine, a delightful and flavorful dish perfect for brunch, lunch, or dinner!

Baked Ziti

Ingredients:

- 1 pound (16 ounces) ziti pasta
- 1 tablespoon olive oil
- 1 onion, finely chopped
- 3 cloves garlic, minced
- 1 pound (about 450g) ground beef or Italian sausage (optional)
- 4 cups marinara sauce (homemade or store-bought)
- 1 cup ricotta cheese
- 2 cups shredded mozzarella cheese, divided
- 1/2 cup grated Parmesan cheese, divided
- 1/4 cup chopped fresh basil or parsley
- Salt and black pepper to taste
- Fresh basil leaves for garnish (optional)

Instructions:

1. Preheat Oven:
    - Preheat your oven to 375°F (190°C). Grease a 9x13-inch baking dish with cooking spray or butter.
2. Cook Pasta:
    - Bring a large pot of salted water to a boil. Cook the ziti pasta according to the package instructions until al dente. Drain the pasta and set aside.
3. Prepare Meat Sauce (if using):
    - In a large skillet, heat olive oil over medium heat. Add the chopped onion and minced garlic. Sauté until softened and fragrant, about 3-4 minutes.
    - If using ground beef or Italian sausage, add it to the skillet with the onions and garlic. Cook until browned and cooked through, breaking up the meat with a spoon. Drain any excess fat.
4. Combine Pasta and Sauce:
    - In a large mixing bowl, combine the cooked ziti pasta and marinara sauce. Stir in the cooked meat sauce (if using) until well combined.
5. Assemble Baked Ziti:
    - Spread half of the pasta mixture evenly into the prepared baking dish. Dollop half of the ricotta cheese over the pasta in small spoonfuls. Sprinkle half of the shredded mozzarella cheese and grated Parmesan cheese over the ricotta. Sprinkle half of the chopped basil or parsley on

top. Repeat the layers with the remaining pasta, ricotta, mozzarella, Parmesan, and herbs.

6. Bake:
   - Cover the baking dish with aluminum foil and bake in the preheated oven for 25 minutes.
   - Remove the foil and continue baking for an additional 10-15 minutes, or until the cheese is melted and bubbly, and the edges are golden brown.
7. Serve:
   - Once baked, remove the baked ziti from the oven and let it cool for a few minutes before serving. Garnish with fresh basil leaves if desired.
   - Serve the baked ziti hot, straight from the oven, and enjoy your delicious homemade comfort food!

Baked ziti is a crowd-pleasing dish that's perfect for family gatherings, potlucks, or any occasion when you crave hearty and comforting Italian cuisine.

Fish Tacos

Ingredients:

For the Fish:

- 1 pound (about 450g) firm white fish fillets (such as cod, tilapia, or mahi-mahi)
- 1/2 cup all-purpose flour
- 1 teaspoon ground cumin
- 1 teaspoon smoked paprika
- 1/2 teaspoon garlic powder
- Salt and black pepper to taste
- Vegetable oil for frying

For Assembly:

- 8 small flour or corn tortillas
- Shredded cabbage or lettuce
- Sliced avocado or guacamole
- Sliced radishes
- Chopped cilantro
- Lime wedges
- Salsa or hot sauce for serving

Instructions:

1. Prepare Fish:
    - Pat the fish fillets dry with paper towels. In a shallow dish, combine the all-purpose flour, ground cumin, smoked paprika, garlic powder, salt, and black pepper.
2. Coat Fish:
    - Dredge each fish fillet in the seasoned flour mixture, shaking off any excess.
3. Fry Fish:
    - In a large skillet, heat vegetable oil over medium-high heat. Carefully add the coated fish fillets to the hot oil and fry until golden brown and crispy on both sides, about 3-4 minutes per side, depending on the thickness of the fillets. Transfer the cooked fish to a plate lined with paper towels to drain excess oil.

4. Warm Tortillas:
   - While the fish is frying, warm the tortillas in a dry skillet or in the oven according to the package instructions. Keep them warm until ready to assemble the tacos.
5. Assemble Tacos:
   - To assemble the fish tacos, place a portion of shredded cabbage or lettuce on each warm tortilla.
   - Top with a crispy fish fillet and desired toppings such as sliced avocado or guacamole, sliced radishes, chopped cilantro, and a squeeze of lime juice.
   - Serve the fish tacos with salsa or hot sauce on the side for extra flavor.
6. Serve:
   - Serve the fish tacos immediately while warm, and enjoy the delicious flavors and textures!

Fish tacos are versatile, so feel free to customize them with your favorite toppings and sauces. They're perfect for a quick and satisfying meal any day of the week.

Caesar Salad

Ingredients:

For the Salad:

- 1 large head of romaine lettuce, washed and torn into bite-sized pieces
- 1 cup croutons (store-bought or homemade)
- 1/4 cup grated Parmesan cheese

For the Caesar Dressing:

- 1/2 cup mayonnaise
- 2 tablespoons grated Parmesan cheese
- 2 tablespoons freshly squeezed lemon juice
- 1 tablespoon Dijon mustard
- 1-2 cloves garlic, minced
- 1 teaspoon Worcestershire sauce
- Salt and black pepper to taste
- 2-3 tablespoons water (optional, to thin out dressing)

Instructions:

1. Prepare Croutons (if making homemade):
    - Preheat your oven to 375°F (190°C). Cut day-old bread into cubes and toss them with olive oil, salt, and any desired seasonings (such as garlic powder or Italian seasoning). Spread the bread cubes on a baking sheet and bake for 10-15 minutes, or until golden and crispy. Let them cool before using in the salad.
2. Make Caesar Dressing:
    - In a small bowl, whisk together the mayonnaise, grated Parmesan cheese, lemon juice, Dijon mustard, minced garlic, Worcestershire sauce, salt, and black pepper until smooth and creamy. If the dressing is too thick, you can thin it out with 2-3 tablespoons of water, adjusting to your desired consistency. Taste and adjust seasoning as needed.
3. Assemble Salad:
    - In a large salad bowl, combine the torn romaine lettuce leaves and croutons.

- Pour the Caesar dressing over the salad and toss gently to coat the lettuce and croutons evenly with the dressing.
4. Add Parmesan Cheese:
    - Sprinkle grated Parmesan cheese over the top of the salad.
5. Serve:
    - Serve the Caesar salad immediately, garnished with additional croutons and Parmesan cheese if desired.
6. Enjoy your homemade Caesar salad as a refreshing and flavorful starter or as a light main course! You can also add grilled chicken or shrimp to make it more substantial.

Stuffed Peppers

Ingredients:

- 4 large bell peppers (any color), tops removed and seeds removed
- 1 cup cooked rice (white or brown)
- 1 pound (about 450g) ground beef or turkey
- 1 onion, finely chopped
- 2 cloves garlic, minced
- 1 cup diced tomatoes (fresh or canned)
- 1 cup tomato sauce or marinara sauce
- 1 teaspoon dried oregano
- 1 teaspoon dried basil
- Salt and black pepper to taste
- 1 cup shredded cheese (such as mozzarella or cheddar), divided
- Fresh parsley or basil leaves for garnish (optional)

Instructions:

1. Preheat Oven:
   - Preheat your oven to 375°F (190°C).
2. Prepare Bell Peppers:
   - Cut the tops off the bell peppers and remove the seeds and membranes from the insides. Rinse the peppers under cold water and pat them dry with paper towels.
3. Cook Rice:
   - Cook the rice according to the package instructions until it's tender. Set aside.
4. Cook Meat and Vegetables:
   - In a large skillet, cook the ground beef or turkey over medium heat until browned and cooked through. Drain any excess fat.
   - Add the chopped onion and minced garlic to the skillet with the cooked meat. Cook until the onion is softened and translucent.
5. Combine Ingredients:
   - Stir in the cooked rice, diced tomatoes, tomato sauce, dried oregano, dried basil, salt, and black pepper. Cook for a few more minutes until the mixture is heated through and well combined. Taste and adjust seasoning if needed.
6. Stuff Peppers:

- Spoon the meat and rice mixture evenly into the prepared bell peppers, pressing down gently to fill each pepper. Place the stuffed peppers upright in a baking dish.
7. Bake:
    - Cover the baking dish with aluminum foil and bake in the preheated oven for 30-35 minutes, or until the peppers are tender.
8. Add Cheese and Finish Baking:
    - Remove the foil from the baking dish. Sprinkle shredded cheese over the top of each stuffed pepper.
    - Return the baking dish to the oven and bake, uncovered, for an additional 10-15 minutes, or until the cheese is melted and bubbly.
9. Serve:
    - Once baked, remove the stuffed peppers from the oven. Garnish with fresh parsley or basil leaves if desired. Serve hot, and enjoy your delicious homemade stuffed peppers!

Stuffed peppers are a hearty and satisfying meal that's perfect for a family dinner or meal prep. You can customize the filling with your favorite ingredients and adjust the seasonings to suit your taste preferences.

Chicken Pot Pie

Ingredients:

For the Filling:

- 2 tablespoons butter
- 1 onion, diced
- 2 carrots, diced
- 2 celery stalks, diced
- 2 cloves garlic, minced
- 1/4 cup all-purpose flour
- 2 cups chicken broth
- 1 cup milk or cream
- 2 cups cooked chicken, diced or shredded
- 1 cup frozen peas
- 1 teaspoon dried thyme
- Salt and black pepper to taste

For the Pastry Crust:

- 1 1/4 cups all-purpose flour
- 1/2 teaspoon salt
- 1/2 cup (1 stick) cold unsalted butter, diced
- 3-4 tablespoons ice water

Instructions:

1. Preheat Oven:
    - Preheat your oven to 375°F (190°C).
2. Make Filling:
    - In a large skillet or Dutch oven, melt the butter over medium heat. Add the diced onion, carrots, and celery. Cook, stirring occasionally, until the vegetables are softened, about 5-7 minutes.
    - Add the minced garlic and cook for an additional 1-2 minutes until fragrant.
    - Sprinkle the flour over the vegetables and stir to coat. Cook for 1-2 minutes to remove the raw flour taste.

- Gradually pour in the chicken broth and milk or cream, stirring constantly to prevent lumps from forming. Cook until the mixture thickens and comes to a simmer.
- Stir in the cooked chicken, frozen peas, dried thyme, salt, and black pepper. Simmer for a few more minutes until the peas are heated through and the filling is thick and creamy. Remove from heat.

3. Make Pastry Crust:
   - In a food processor, combine the flour and salt. Add the diced cold butter and pulse until the mixture resembles coarse crumbs.
   - Gradually add the ice water, 1 tablespoon at a time, pulsing until the dough comes together and forms a ball. Be careful not to overwork the dough.
   - Flatten the dough into a disk, wrap it in plastic wrap, and refrigerate for at least 30 minutes.

4. Assemble Pot Pie:
   - Transfer the chicken filling to a 9-inch pie dish or baking dish.
   - On a lightly floured surface, roll out the chilled dough into a circle slightly larger than the diameter of the pie dish. Place the rolled-out dough over the filling, tucking the edges under and crimping as desired. Cut a few slits in the center of the crust to allow steam to escape.

5. Bake:
   - Place the assembled pot pie on a baking sheet to catch any drips. Bake in the preheated oven for 30-35 minutes, or until the crust is golden brown and the filling is bubbly.

6. Serve:
   - Once baked, remove the chicken pot pie from the oven and let it cool for a few minutes before serving. Slice and serve hot, and enjoy the comforting flavors of homemade chicken pot pie!

Chicken pot pie is a classic comfort food that's perfect for a cozy family dinner or special occasion. Adjust the vegetables and seasonings to suit your taste preferences.

Beef Bourguignon

Ingredients:

- 2 pounds (about 900g) beef chuck or stewing beef, cut into 1-inch cubes
- Salt and black pepper to taste
- 3 tablespoons all-purpose flour
- 3 tablespoons olive oil or vegetable oil, divided
- 6 slices bacon, chopped
- 1 onion, chopped
- 2 carrots, peeled and sliced
- 2 cloves garlic, minced
- 1 tablespoon tomato paste
- 2 cups red wine (such as Burgundy or Pinot Noir)
- 2 cups beef broth
- 1 bouquet garni (a bundle of fresh herbs such as thyme, parsley, and bay leaves tied together with kitchen twine)
- 1 pound (about 450g) mushrooms, quartered
- Chopped fresh parsley for garnish (optional)

Instructions:

1. Preheat Oven:
    - Preheat your oven to 325°F (160°C).
2. Season and Flour Beef:
    - Season the beef cubes generously with salt and black pepper. Dredge the beef cubes in the flour, shaking off any excess.
3. Brown Beef:
    - In a large Dutch oven or oven-safe pot, heat 2 tablespoons of oil over medium-high heat. Add the beef cubes in batches and cook until browned on all sides, about 4-5 minutes per batch. Transfer the browned beef to a plate and set aside.
4. Cook Bacon and Vegetables:
    - In the same pot, add the chopped bacon and cook until crispy. Remove the bacon from the pot and set aside, leaving the rendered fat in the pot.
    - Add the chopped onion and sliced carrots to the pot. Cook, stirring occasionally, until the vegetables are softened, about 5 minutes. Add the minced garlic and cook for an additional 1-2 minutes.
5. Deglaze and Simmer:

- Stir in the tomato paste and cook for 1 minute. Pour in the red wine, scraping up any browned bits from the bottom of the pot. Bring the mixture to a simmer and cook for 5 minutes to reduce slightly.
- Return the browned beef cubes and crispy bacon to the pot. Add the beef broth and bouquet garni. Bring the mixture to a simmer.

6. Braise in Oven:
    - Cover the pot with a lid and transfer it to the preheated oven. Braise the beef bourguignon in the oven for 2 to 2 1/2 hours, or until the beef is tender and the flavors have melded together.

7. Sauté Mushrooms:
    - In a separate skillet, heat the remaining 1 tablespoon of oil over medium-high heat. Add the quartered mushrooms and cook until golden brown and tender, about 5-7 minutes. Season with salt and black pepper to taste.

8. Finish and Serve:
    - Remove the pot from the oven. Discard the bouquet garni. Stir in the sautéed mushrooms.
    - Taste and adjust seasoning with salt and black pepper if needed. Garnish with chopped fresh parsley if desired.
    - Serve the beef bourguignon hot, accompanied by crusty bread, mashed potatoes, or cooked egg noodles.

Beef bourguignon is a rich and flavorful dish that's perfect for a special occasion or a comforting meal on a chilly day. Enjoy the complex flavors of this classic French stew!

Vegetable Curry

Ingredients:

For the Curry Paste:

- 2 cloves garlic, minced
- 1 tablespoon grated fresh ginger
- 1 small onion, chopped
- 2 tablespoons curry powder
- 1 teaspoon ground cumin
- 1 teaspoon ground coriander
- 1/2 teaspoon turmeric powder
- 1/4 teaspoon cayenne pepper (optional, for heat)
- 2 tablespoons tomato paste
- 1/4 cup vegetable broth or water

For the Vegetable Curry:

- 2 tablespoons vegetable oil
- 1 small onion, thinly sliced
- 2 carrots, peeled and sliced
- 2 potatoes, peeled and diced
- 1 bell pepper, diced
- 1 cup cauliflower florets
- 1 cup broccoli florets
- 1 can (14 ounces) chickpeas, drained and rinsed
- 1 can (14 ounces) coconut milk
- Salt and black pepper to taste
- Fresh cilantro leaves for garnish (optional)
- Cooked rice or naan bread for serving

Instructions:

1. Prepare Curry Paste:
    - In a small bowl, mix together the minced garlic, grated ginger, chopped onion, curry powder, ground cumin, ground coriander, turmeric powder, cayenne pepper (if using), tomato paste, and vegetable broth or water. Stir until well combined to form a paste. Set aside.

2. Cook Vegetables:
   - Heat the vegetable oil in a large skillet or pot over medium heat. Add the thinly sliced onion and cook until softened, about 2-3 minutes.
   - Add the sliced carrots and diced potatoes to the skillet. Cook for another 5 minutes, stirring occasionally, until the vegetables start to soften.
3. Add Curry Paste:
   - Push the vegetables to one side of the skillet and add the curry paste to the empty side. Cook the paste for about 1 minute, stirring constantly, until fragrant.
4. Combine and Simmer:
   - Mix the curry paste with the vegetables in the skillet until evenly coated. Add the diced bell pepper, cauliflower florets, broccoli florets, and drained chickpeas to the skillet. Stir to combine.
   - Pour the coconut milk into the skillet and stir well to combine all the ingredients. Season with salt and black pepper to taste.
5. Simmer Curry:
   - Bring the curry to a simmer, then reduce the heat to low. Cover the skillet and let the curry simmer gently for about 15-20 minutes, or until the vegetables are tender and the flavors have melded together.
6. Serve:
   - Once cooked, remove the skillet from the heat. Taste and adjust seasoning if needed. Garnish with fresh cilantro leaves if desired.
   - Serve the vegetable curry hot, accompanied by cooked rice or warm naan bread.

Enjoy your homemade vegetable curry, a delicious and nutritious dish that's perfect for vegetarians and vegans alike! Feel free to customize the vegetables and spices according to your taste preferences.

BBQ Ribs

Ingredients:

For the Ribs:

- 2 racks of baby back ribs (about 2-3 pounds each)
- Salt and black pepper to taste

For the Dry Rub:

- 2 tablespoons brown sugar
- 1 tablespoon smoked paprika
- 1 tablespoon garlic powder
- 1 tablespoon onion powder
- 1 teaspoon chili powder
- 1 teaspoon ground cumin
- 1 teaspoon ground mustard
- 1 teaspoon salt
- 1/2 teaspoon black pepper

For the BBQ Sauce:

- 1 cup ketchup
- 1/4 cup apple cider vinegar
- 1/4 cup brown sugar
- 2 tablespoons honey
- 2 tablespoons Worcestershire sauce
- 1 tablespoon Dijon mustard
- 1 teaspoon smoked paprika
- 1 teaspoon garlic powder
- Salt and black pepper to taste

Instructions:

1. Prepare Ribs:
    - Preheat your oven to 275°F (135°C). Line a baking sheet with aluminum foil for easy cleanup.

- Remove the membrane from the back of the ribs if it's still attached. Season the ribs generously with salt and black pepper.
2. Make Dry Rub:
    - In a small bowl, combine all the dry rub ingredients: brown sugar, smoked paprika, garlic powder, onion powder, chili powder, ground cumin, ground mustard, salt, and black pepper. Mix well.
3. Rub Ribs:
    - Rub the dry rub mixture evenly over the surface of the ribs, covering both sides.
4. Wrap Ribs:
    - Place each rack of ribs on a large piece of heavy-duty aluminum foil. Wrap tightly, sealing the edges to prevent any leaks.
5. Bake Ribs:
    - Place the wrapped ribs on the prepared baking sheet. Bake in the preheated oven for 2.5 to 3 hours, or until the ribs are tender and the meat starts to pull away from the bones.
6. Make BBQ Sauce:
    - While the ribs are baking, prepare the BBQ sauce. In a saucepan, combine all the BBQ sauce ingredients: ketchup, apple cider vinegar, brown sugar, honey, Worcestershire sauce, Dijon mustard, smoked paprika, garlic powder, salt, and black pepper. Bring to a simmer over medium heat, then reduce the heat and let the sauce simmer for 10-15 minutes, stirring occasionally, until it thickens slightly.
7. Finish Ribs:
    - Once the ribs are tender, carefully remove them from the foil and place them back on the baking sheet. Brush the ribs generously with the prepared BBQ sauce, coating them evenly.
8. Broil Ribs:
    - Turn on the broiler in your oven. Place the ribs under the broiler for 3-5 minutes, or until the BBQ sauce caramelizes and forms a sticky glaze. Watch carefully to prevent burning.
9. Serve:
    - Once glazed, remove the ribs from the oven. Let them rest for a few minutes before slicing between the bones and serving hot.

Enjoy your homemade oven-baked BBQ ribs with your favorite sides like coleslaw, cornbread, or baked beans for a delicious and satisfying meal!

Lobster Bisque

Ingredients:

- 2 lobsters (about 1 1/2 to 2 pounds each)
- 4 tablespoons unsalted butter
- 1 onion, chopped
- 2 carrots, chopped
- 2 celery stalks, chopped
- 2 cloves garlic, minced
- 2 tablespoons tomato paste
- 1/4 cup all-purpose flour
- 1 cup dry white wine
- 4 cups seafood broth or chicken broth
- 2 cups water
- 1 bay leaf
- 1 teaspoon dried thyme
- 1/2 teaspoon paprika
- 1 cup heavy cream
- Salt and black pepper to taste
- Chopped fresh parsley or chives for garnish (optional)

Instructions:

1. Prepare Lobsters:
    - Bring a large pot of salted water to a boil. Add the lobsters and cook for about 8-10 minutes, or until they turn bright red and are cooked through. Remove the lobsters from the pot and let them cool slightly. Reserve the cooking liquid to use as broth for the bisque.
2. Extract Meat:
    - Once the lobsters are cool enough to handle, remove the meat from the shells. Chop the lobster meat into bite-sized pieces and set aside. Reserve the shells for making broth.
3. Make Broth:
    - In a large pot, melt 2 tablespoons of butter over medium heat. Add the chopped onion, carrots, celery, and garlic. Cook, stirring occasionally, until the vegetables are softened, about 5-7 minutes.

- Stir in the tomato paste and cook for another 2 minutes. Sprinkle the flour over the vegetables and cook, stirring constantly, for 1-2 minutes to make a roux.
- Gradually pour in the white wine, scraping up any browned bits from the bottom of the pot. Cook for 2-3 minutes to reduce slightly.
- Add the seafood broth (or chicken broth), water, reserved lobster shells, bay leaf, dried thyme, and paprika to the pot. Bring the mixture to a simmer, then reduce the heat to low. Cover and simmer for 30-45 minutes to infuse the flavors.

4. Strain Broth:
   - Once the broth is flavored, strain it through a fine mesh sieve into a clean pot, discarding the solids. Return the strained broth to the pot.
5. Make Bisque:
   - Stir in the chopped lobster meat and heavy cream into the strained broth. Season with salt and black pepper to taste. Bring the bisque to a gentle simmer over low heat, stirring occasionally, for 10-15 minutes to heat through and allow the flavors to meld together.
6. Serve:
   - Once heated through, remove the lobster bisque from the heat. Ladle the bisque into bowls and garnish with chopped fresh parsley or chives if desired. Serve hot, and enjoy the luxurious flavors of homemade lobster bisque!

Lobster bisque is a decadent soup that's perfect for special occasions or when you want to treat yourself to a gourmet meal at home. Serve it with crusty bread or oyster crackers for dipping.

Shepherd's Pie

Ingredients:

For the Mashed Potatoes:

- 2 pounds (about 900g) potatoes, peeled and cut into chunks
- 4 tablespoons unsalted butter
- 1/2 cup milk or cream
- Salt and black pepper to taste

For the Meat Filling:

- 1 tablespoon olive oil
- 1 onion, chopped
- 2 carrots, diced
- 2 cloves garlic, minced
- 1 pound (about 450g) ground beef or lamb
- 2 tablespoons all-purpose flour
- 1 cup beef or vegetable broth
- 1 tablespoon tomato paste
- 1 tablespoon Worcestershire sauce
- 1 teaspoon dried thyme
- 1 cup frozen peas
- Salt and black pepper to taste

Instructions:

1. Preheat Oven:
    - Preheat your oven to 375°F (190°C). Grease a 9x13-inch baking dish with butter or cooking spray.
2. Make Mashed Potatoes:
    - Place the peeled and chopped potatoes in a large pot of salted water. Bring to a boil and cook until the potatoes are fork-tender, about 15-20 minutes.
    - Drain the cooked potatoes and return them to the pot. Add the butter and milk or cream. Mash the potatoes until smooth and creamy. Season with salt and black pepper to taste. Set aside.
3. Prepare Meat Filling:

- In a large skillet, heat the olive oil over medium heat. Add the chopped onion and diced carrots. Cook, stirring occasionally, until the vegetables are softened, about 5-7 minutes.
- Add the minced garlic and cook for an additional minute until fragrant.
- Add the ground beef or lamb to the skillet. Cook, breaking up the meat with a spoon, until browned and cooked through.
- Sprinkle the flour over the meat and vegetables. Stir well to combine and cook for 1-2 minutes.
- Pour in the beef or vegetable broth, tomato paste, Worcestershire sauce, and dried thyme. Stir to combine and bring the mixture to a simmer. Cook for a few minutes until the sauce thickens slightly.
- Stir in the frozen peas. Season the meat filling with salt and black pepper to taste. Remove from heat.

4. Assemble Shepherd's Pie:
   - Transfer the meat filling to the prepared baking dish, spreading it out into an even layer.
   - Spread the mashed potatoes over the top of the meat filling, smoothing it out with a spatula.
5. Bake:
   - Place the assembled shepherd's pie in the preheated oven. Bake for 25-30 minutes, or until the mashed potatoes are golden brown and the filling is bubbly.
6. Serve:
   - Once baked, remove the shepherd's pie from the oven and let it cool for a few minutes before serving.
   - Serve the shepherd's pie hot, and enjoy the comforting flavors of this classic dish!

Shepherd's pie is a hearty and satisfying meal that's perfect for a cozy dinner with family and friends. Feel free to customize the recipe by adding other vegetables or herbs to the filling according to your taste preferences.

Shakshuka

Ingredients:

- 2 tablespoons olive oil
- 1 onion, diced
- 1 red bell pepper, diced
- 1 yellow bell pepper, diced
- 2 cloves garlic, minced
- 1 teaspoon ground cumin
- 1 teaspoon smoked paprika
- 1/2 teaspoon chili powder (adjust to taste)
- 1 can (14 ounces) diced tomatoes
- Salt and black pepper to taste
- 4-6 large eggs
- Fresh parsley or cilantro for garnish (optional)
- Crumbled feta cheese for garnish (optional)
- Crusty bread or pita for serving

Instructions:

1. Sauté Vegetables:
    - Heat the olive oil in a large skillet or cast-iron pan over medium heat. Add the diced onion and bell peppers. Cook, stirring occasionally, until the vegetables are softened, about 5-7 minutes.
2. Add Aromatics and Spices:
    - Add the minced garlic, ground cumin, smoked paprika, and chili powder to the skillet. Cook for an additional 1-2 minutes until fragrant.
3. Simmer Sauce:
    - Pour the diced tomatoes into the skillet, including their juices. Stir well to combine. Season the sauce with salt and black pepper to taste. Simmer the sauce for 10-15 minutes, or until it has thickened slightly.
4. Make Wells for Eggs:
    - Using a spoon, create small wells or indentations in the tomato sauce for the eggs. Crack one egg into each well, being careful not to break the yolks.
5. Poach Eggs:

- Cover the skillet and let the eggs cook in the simmering sauce for 5-7 minutes, or until the egg whites are set but the yolks are still runny. Cook longer if you prefer firmer yolks.
6. Garnish and Serve:
    - Once the eggs are cooked to your liking, remove the skillet from heat. Garnish the shakshuka with chopped fresh parsley or cilantro and crumbled feta cheese, if desired.
    - Serve the shakshuka hot, straight from the skillet, with crusty bread or pita for dipping into the sauce and soaking up the runny egg yolks.

Shakshuka makes for a delicious and satisfying breakfast, brunch, or dinner option. It's flavorful, comforting, and perfect for sharing with family and friends. Feel free to adjust the level of spiciness according to your taste preferences by adding more or less chili powder. Enjoy!

Chicken Marsala

Ingredients:

- 4 boneless, skinless chicken breasts
- Salt and black pepper to taste
- 1/2 cup all-purpose flour, for dredging
- 4 tablespoons unsalted butter, divided
- 2 tablespoons olive oil
- 8 ounces (about 225g) cremini or button mushrooms, sliced
- 2 cloves garlic, minced
- 1 cup Marsala wine
- 1 cup chicken broth
- 2 tablespoons chopped fresh parsley, for garnish (optional)

Instructions:

1. Prepare Chicken:
   - Place each chicken breast between two sheets of plastic wrap and pound with a meat mallet or rolling pin until about 1/4 inch thick. Season both sides of the chicken breasts with salt and black pepper.
2. Dredge Chicken:
   - Dredge the seasoned chicken breasts in the flour, shaking off any excess.
3. Cook Chicken:
   - In a large skillet, heat 2 tablespoons of butter and 2 tablespoons of olive oil over medium-high heat. Add the dredged chicken breasts to the skillet and cook until golden brown on both sides and cooked through, about 3-4 minutes per side. Transfer the cooked chicken to a plate and set aside.
4. Sauté Mushrooms and Garlic:
   - In the same skillet, add the remaining 2 tablespoons of butter. Add the sliced mushrooms and minced garlic to the skillet. Cook, stirring occasionally, until the mushrooms are golden brown and softened, about 5-7 minutes.
5. Make Marsala Sauce:
   - Pour the Marsala wine into the skillet, scraping up any browned bits from the bottom with a wooden spoon. Let the wine simmer for 1-2 minutes to reduce slightly.
   - Stir in the chicken broth and bring the mixture to a simmer. Cook for another 5-7 minutes, allowing the sauce to thicken.

6. Add Chicken Back to Skillet:
    - Return the cooked chicken breasts to the skillet, nestling them into the sauce. Simmer for an additional 2-3 minutes to heat the chicken through and allow it to absorb some of the flavors of the sauce.
7. Garnish and Serve:
    - Once heated through, remove the skillet from heat. Garnish the Chicken Marsala with chopped fresh parsley, if desired.
    - Serve the Chicken Marsala hot, accompanied by pasta, rice, or mashed potatoes, and your favorite vegetables.

Enjoy your homemade Chicken Marsala, a delicious and elegant dish that's perfect for a special dinner at home!

Eggplant Parmesan

Ingredients:

For the Eggplant:

- 2 large eggplants
- Salt
- 2 cups breadcrumbs (plain or seasoned)
- 1 cup all-purpose flour
- 4 large eggs, beaten
- Olive oil, for frying

For Assembly:

- 2 cups marinara sauce (homemade or store-bought)
- 2 cups shredded mozzarella cheese
- 1/2 cup grated Parmesan cheese
- Fresh basil leaves, chopped (for garnish, optional)

Instructions:

1. Preheat Oven:
    - Preheat your oven to 375°F (190°C). Grease a baking dish with olive oil or non-stick cooking spray.
2. Prepare Eggplant:
    - Slice the eggplants into 1/4-inch thick rounds. Place the slices in a colander and sprinkle them generously with salt. Let the eggplant slices sit for about 30 minutes to release excess moisture. After 30 minutes, rinse the eggplant slices under cold water and pat them dry with paper towels.
3. Bread Eggplant:
    - Set up a breading station with three shallow dishes: one with flour, one with beaten eggs, and one with breadcrumbs.
    - Dip each eggplant slice first in the flour, shaking off any excess, then in the beaten eggs, and finally in the breadcrumbs, pressing gently to adhere. Place the breaded eggplant slices on a baking sheet in a single layer.
4. Fry Eggplant:
    - In a large skillet, heat about 1/4 inch of olive oil over medium-high heat. Working in batches, fry the breaded eggplant slices until golden brown on

both sides, about 2-3 minutes per side. Transfer the fried eggplant slices to a plate lined with paper towels to drain excess oil.
5. Assemble Eggplant Parmesan:
    - Spread a thin layer of marinara sauce on the bottom of the prepared baking dish. Arrange a layer of fried eggplant slices on top of the sauce, overlapping slightly if needed.
    - Spoon marinara sauce over the eggplant slices, followed by a layer of shredded mozzarella cheese and grated Parmesan cheese. Repeat the layers until all the eggplant slices are used, finishing with a layer of marinara sauce and cheese on top.
6. Bake:
    - Cover the baking dish with aluminum foil and bake in the preheated oven for 25-30 minutes, or until the cheese is melted and bubbly.
7. Serve:
    - Once baked, remove the foil from the baking dish. Let the Eggplant Parmesan cool for a few minutes before slicing.
    - Garnish with chopped fresh basil leaves, if desired, and serve hot.

Enjoy your homemade Eggplant Parmesan, a delicious and comforting dish that's perfect for a vegetarian main course or a side dish with pasta or salad!

Paella

Ingredients:

- 2 cups short-grain Spanish rice (such as Bomba or Calasparra)
- 4 cups chicken broth (or seafood broth)
- 1/4 cup olive oil
- 1 onion, finely chopped
- 4 cloves garlic, minced
- 1 red bell pepper, diced
- 1 green bell pepper, diced
- 1 tomato, diced
- 1 teaspoon smoked paprika
- 1/2 teaspoon saffron threads
- 1 pound (about 450g) mixed seafood (such as shrimp, squid, mussels, and clams)
- 1/2 pound (about 225g) Spanish chorizo, sliced
- 1/2 cup frozen peas
- Salt and black pepper to taste
- Lemon wedges for serving
- Chopped fresh parsley for garnish

Instructions:

1. Prepare Ingredients:
    - Rinse the rice under cold water until the water runs clear. Set aside.
    - Warm the chicken broth in a saucepan over low heat. Keep it warm while preparing the other ingredients.
2. Sauté Aromatics:
    - In a large paella pan or skillet, heat the olive oil over medium heat. Add the chopped onion and sauté until softened, about 3-4 minutes.
    - Add the minced garlic, diced bell peppers, and diced tomato to the pan. Cook, stirring occasionally, until the vegetables are tender, about 5-6 minutes.
3. Add Seasonings:
    - Stir in the smoked paprika and saffron threads, and cook for another minute until fragrant.
4. Cook Rice:

- Add the rinsed rice to the pan, stirring to coat it with the oil and vegetables. Cook for 1-2 minutes to lightly toast the rice.
- Pour the warm chicken broth into the pan, stirring to combine. Bring the mixture to a simmer.

5. Arrange Seafood and Chorizo:
   - Arrange the mixed seafood and sliced chorizo over the rice mixture in the pan. Gently press the seafood and chorizo into the rice.
6. Simmer:
   - Reduce the heat to low and let the paella simmer, uncovered, for 20-25 minutes, or until the rice is tender and the liquid is absorbed. Avoid stirring the paella once the broth has been added to allow the characteristic socarrat (crispy bottom layer) to form.
7. Add Peas:
   - Sprinkle the frozen peas over the paella during the last few minutes of cooking. Cover the pan and cook until the peas are heated through.
8. Garnish and Serve:
   - Once the paella is cooked, remove it from the heat. Let it rest, covered, for a few minutes.
   - Garnish the paella with chopped fresh parsley and serve hot, accompanied by lemon wedges for squeezing over the rice.

Enjoy your homemade paella, a delicious and festive dish that's perfect for sharing with family and friends!

Chicken Cordon Bleu

Ingredients:

- 4 boneless, skinless chicken breasts
- Salt and black pepper to taste
- 4 slices Swiss cheese
- 4 slices deli ham
- 1/2 cup all-purpose flour
- 2 large eggs, beaten
- 1 cup breadcrumbs (plain or seasoned)
- 2 tablespoons olive oil or melted butter
- Toothpicks (optional, for securing)

Instructions:

1. Preheat Oven:
    - Preheat your oven to 375°F (190°C). Grease a baking dish with olive oil or non-stick cooking spray.
2. Prepare Chicken:
    - Place each chicken breast between two sheets of plastic wrap or wax paper. Use a meat mallet or rolling pin to pound the chicken breasts to an even thickness of about 1/4 inch. Season both sides of the chicken breasts with salt and black pepper.
3. Assemble Chicken Cordon Bleu:
    - Place a slice of Swiss cheese and a slice of deli ham on each chicken breast.
    - Starting from the narrow end of each chicken breast, roll up the chicken tightly, enclosing the cheese and ham inside. If necessary, secure the rolls with toothpicks to hold them together.
4. Coat Chicken:
    - Set up a breading station with three shallow dishes: one with flour, one with beaten eggs, and one with breadcrumbs.
    - Dip each chicken roll first in the flour, shaking off any excess, then in the beaten eggs, and finally in the breadcrumbs, pressing gently to coat evenly.
5. Cook Chicken:

- In a large skillet, heat the olive oil or melted butter over medium-high heat. Add the breaded chicken rolls to the skillet, seam side down, and cook until golden brown on all sides, about 3-4 minutes per side.

6. Bake Chicken:
    - Transfer the browned chicken rolls to the prepared baking dish. Bake in the preheated oven for 20-25 minutes, or until the chicken is cooked through and the cheese is melted and bubbly.
7. Serve:
    - Once baked, remove the chicken from the oven and let it rest for a few minutes. Remove any toothpicks before serving.
    - Serve the Chicken Cordon Bleu hot, accompanied by your favorite sides such as mashed potatoes, steamed vegetables, or a crisp green salad.

Enjoy your homemade Chicken Cordon Bleu, a delicious and elegant dish that's perfect for a special dinner at home!

Gumbo

Ingredients:

For the Roux:

- 1/2 cup all-purpose flour
- 1/2 cup vegetable oil

For the Gumbo:

- 1 pound boneless, skinless chicken thighs, diced
- 1/2 pound Andouille sausage, sliced
- 1 large onion, diced
- 1 bell pepper, diced
- 2 celery stalks, diced
- 4 cloves garlic, minced
- 4 cups chicken broth
- 1 can (14.5 ounces) diced tomatoes
- 1 cup okra, sliced (fresh or frozen)
- 2 bay leaves
- 1 teaspoon dried thyme
- 1 teaspoon paprika
- 1/2 teaspoon cayenne pepper (adjust to taste)
- Salt and black pepper to taste
- Cooked white rice for serving
- Chopped green onions for garnish
- Hot sauce (optional, for serving)

Instructions:

1. Make Roux:
    - In a large, heavy-bottomed pot or Dutch oven, heat the vegetable oil over medium heat. Gradually whisk in the flour to create a smooth paste. Cook, stirring constantly, for 20-30 minutes or until the roux reaches a dark chocolate color. Be careful not to burn it.
2. Cook Chicken and Sausage:
    - Once the roux is darkened, add the diced chicken thighs to the pot. Cook, stirring occasionally, until the chicken is browned on all sides.

- Add the sliced Andouille sausage to the pot and cook for an additional 5 minutes, allowing it to brown slightly.
3. Sauté Aromatics:
    - Add the diced onion, bell pepper, celery, and minced garlic to the pot. Cook, stirring occasionally, until the vegetables are softened, about 5-7 minutes.
4. Add Broth and Seasonings:
    - Pour in the chicken broth and diced tomatoes with their juices. Add the sliced okra, bay leaves, dried thyme, paprika, cayenne pepper, salt, and black pepper to taste. Stir well to combine.
5. Simmer Gumbo:
    - Bring the gumbo to a simmer over medium heat. Reduce the heat to low, cover, and let it simmer gently for 45 minutes to 1 hour, stirring occasionally, until the flavors meld together and the gumbo thickens.
6. Serve:
    - Once the gumbo is cooked and thickened to your liking, remove the bay leaves and discard them.
    - Serve the gumbo hot over cooked white rice.
    - Garnish each serving with chopped green onions and offer hot sauce on the side for those who like it spicier.

Enjoy your homemade chicken and sausage gumbo, a comforting and flavorful dish perfect for cold days or anytime you're craving a taste of Louisiana cuisine!

Falafel

Ingredients:

For the Falafel:

- 1 cup dried chickpeas, soaked overnight (or 2 cans, drained and rinsed)
- 1 small onion, chopped
- 3 cloves garlic, minced
- 1/4 cup fresh parsley, chopped
- 1/4 cup fresh cilantro, chopped
- 1 teaspoon ground cumin
- 1 teaspoon ground coriander
- 1/4 teaspoon cayenne pepper (optional, for heat)
- 1 teaspoon salt, or to taste
- 1/2 teaspoon black pepper
- 1/2 teaspoon baking soda
- 2-3 tablespoons all-purpose flour, if needed
- Vegetable oil for frying

For Serving:

- Pita bread or flatbread
- Hummus
- Tahini sauce
- Chopped lettuce, tomatoes, cucumbers
- Pickled vegetables (such as turnips or cucumbers)
- Chopped fresh parsley or cilantro
- Lemon wedges

Instructions:

1. Prepare Chickpeas:
    - If using dried chickpeas, soak them in water overnight. Drain and rinse well before using. If using canned chickpeas, drain and rinse them thoroughly.
2. Make Falafel Mixture:
    - In a food processor, combine the soaked and drained chickpeas, chopped onion, minced garlic, fresh parsley, fresh cilantro, ground cumin, ground coriander, cayenne pepper (if using), salt, black pepper, and baking soda.

Pulse until the mixture is coarse and crumbly, but holds together when pressed. Avoid over-processing; you want some texture.
- If the mixture is too wet to hold its shape, add 2-3 tablespoons of all-purpose flour and pulse again until combined.

3. Form Falafel Balls:
   - Use your hands to shape the falafel mixture into small balls or patties, about 1 1/2 inches in diameter. Place the formed falafel on a baking sheet lined with parchment paper.
4. Fry Falafel:
   - In a large skillet or deep fryer, heat vegetable oil to 350°F (175°C). Carefully add the falafel to the hot oil in batches, making sure not to overcrowd the pan. Fry until golden brown and crispy, about 3-4 minutes per side. Use a slotted spoon to transfer the fried falafel to a plate lined with paper towels to drain excess oil.
5. Serve:
   - Serve the falafel hot, stuffed into warm pita bread or flatbread. Top with hummus, tahini sauce, chopped lettuce, tomatoes, cucumbers, pickled vegetables, and chopped fresh parsley or cilantro. Squeeze lemon juice over the falafel for extra flavor.
   - Falafel can also be served as part of a mezze platter or salad.

Enjoy your homemade falafel, a delicious and satisfying dish that's perfect for lunch, dinner, or as a snack!

Sushi Rolls

Ingredients:

For the Sushi Rice:

- 1 cup sushi rice (short-grain Japanese rice)
- 1 1/4 cups water
- 2 tablespoons rice vinegar
- 1 tablespoon sugar
- 1/2 teaspoon salt

For the Sushi Rolls:

- Nori (seaweed) sheets
- Sushi rice
- Fillings of your choice (e.g., sliced raw fish, cooked shrimp, avocado, cucumber, carrot, cream cheese, crab sticks)
- Soy sauce, for serving
- Pickled ginger, for serving
- Wasabi, for serving

Instructions:

1. Prepare Sushi Rice:
    - Rinse the sushi rice under cold water until the water runs clear. Combine the rinsed rice and water in a rice cooker or pot and cook according to the rice cooker instructions or on the stovetop until the rice is cooked and slightly sticky.
    - In a small saucepan, heat the rice vinegar, sugar, and salt over low heat until the sugar and salt dissolve. Once the rice is cooked, transfer it to a large bowl and gently fold in the seasoned vinegar mixture. Let the rice cool to room temperature.
2. Prepare Fillings:
    - Prepare your fillings by slicing them into thin strips. Common fillings include raw fish, cooked shrimp, avocado, cucumber, carrot, cream cheese, and crab sticks.
3. Assemble Sushi Rolls:

- Place a nori sheet on a bamboo sushi mat or a clean kitchen towel. With wet hands, spread a thin layer of sushi rice evenly over the nori sheet, leaving a 1-inch border at the top edge.
- Arrange your desired fillings horizontally across the center of the rice-covered nori sheet.
- Using the bamboo mat or towel, tightly roll up the sushi from the bottom edge, applying gentle pressure to shape it into a cylinder. Wet the top border of the nori sheet with a little water to seal the roll.
- Repeat the process with the remaining nori sheets and fillings.

4. Slice and Serve:
   - Use a sharp knife dipped in water to slice the sushi rolls into 6-8 pieces each.
   - Serve the sushi rolls with soy sauce, pickled ginger, and wasabi on the side.
5. Enjoy:
   - Enjoy your homemade sushi rolls as a delicious snack, appetizer, or main dish!

Feel free to get creative with your sushi rolls by experimenting with different fillings, sauces, and toppings. Once you get the hang of rolling sushi, you can try making more intricate rolls like inside-out rolls (uramaki) or specialty rolls with unique combinations of ingredients.

Beef Chili

Ingredients:

- 1 tablespoon olive oil
- 1 onion, chopped
- 3 cloves garlic, minced
- 1 pound ground beef (lean)
- 1 can (14.5 ounces) diced tomatoes
- 1 can (15 ounces) kidney beans, drained and rinsed
- 1 can (15 ounces) black beans, drained and rinsed
- 1 can (6 ounces) tomato paste
- 2 cups beef broth
- 2 tablespoons chili powder
- 1 teaspoon ground cumin
- 1 teaspoon paprika
- 1/2 teaspoon dried oregano
- 1/2 teaspoon salt, or to taste
- 1/4 teaspoon black pepper
- Optional toppings: shredded cheese, sour cream, sliced jalapeños, chopped cilantro, diced avocado

Instructions:

1. Sauté Aromatics:
    - Heat olive oil in a large pot or Dutch oven over medium heat. Add chopped onion and minced garlic. Cook, stirring occasionally, until the onion is softened and translucent, about 5 minutes.
2. Brown Ground Beef:
    - Add ground beef to the pot. Break it up with a spoon and cook until browned, stirring occasionally, about 5-7 minutes.
3. Add Tomatoes and Beans:
    - Stir in diced tomatoes, kidney beans, black beans, and tomato paste. Mix well to combine.
4. Season and Simmer:
    - Pour in beef broth and add chili powder, ground cumin, paprika, dried oregano, salt, and black pepper. Stir to incorporate the seasonings.

- Bring the chili to a simmer, then reduce the heat to low. Cover and let it simmer for about 30 minutes to allow the flavors to meld together, stirring occasionally.
5. Adjust Seasoning:
    - Taste the chili and adjust seasoning if needed. Add more salt or spices according to your preference.
6. Serve:
    - Ladle the beef chili into bowls. Serve hot with optional toppings such as shredded cheese, sour cream, sliced jalapeños, chopped cilantro, or diced avocado.
7. Enjoy:
    - Enjoy your homemade beef chili as a comforting and satisfying meal!

Feel free to customize this basic beef chili recipe by adding additional ingredients such as bell peppers, corn, or different types of beans. You can also adjust the level of spiciness by adding more or less chili powder or adding diced green chilies.

Gazpacho

Ingredients:

- 6 ripe tomatoes, chopped
- 1 cucumber, peeled and chopped
- 1 bell pepper (red, yellow, or green), seeded and chopped
- 1 small red onion, chopped
- 2 cloves garlic, minced
- 2 slices day-old bread, crusts removed and soaked in water
- 1/4 cup extra-virgin olive oil
- 2 tablespoons red wine vinegar
- 1 teaspoon salt, or to taste
- 1/4 teaspoon black pepper, or to taste
- Optional toppings: diced cucumber, bell pepper, red onion, croutons, fresh herbs (such as parsley or cilantro), drizzle of olive oil

Instructions:

1. Prepare Vegetables:
   - In a large bowl, combine the chopped tomatoes, cucumber, bell pepper, red onion, and minced garlic.
2. Soak Bread:
   - Remove the crusts from the slices of day-old bread and tear the bread into small pieces. Place the bread in a bowl of water and let it soak for about 5 minutes.
3. Blend Ingredients:
   - Squeeze out excess water from the soaked bread and add the bread to the bowl of chopped vegetables.
   - Add extra-virgin olive oil, red wine vinegar, salt, and black pepper to the bowl.
   - Using an immersion blender or a regular blender, blend the ingredients until smooth and creamy. If using a regular blender, you may need to blend in batches.
   - Taste the gazpacho and adjust the seasoning if needed, adding more salt, vinegar, or pepper according to your preference.
4. Chill:

- Cover the gazpacho and refrigerate for at least 1 hour to chill and allow the flavors to meld together. You can also chill it overnight for even better flavor.
5. Serve:
    - Stir the gazpacho well before serving. Ladle the chilled soup into bowls.
    - Garnish with diced cucumber, bell pepper, red onion, croutons, fresh herbs, and a drizzle of olive oil, if desired.
6. Enjoy:
    - Serve the gazpacho cold as a refreshing appetizer or light meal, especially on hot summer days.

Gazpacho is a versatile dish, and you can adjust the ingredients and seasoning to suit your taste preferences. Feel free to add more vegetables or herbs, or adjust the texture by blending it to your desired consistency.

Lamb Kebabs

Ingredients:

For the Marinade:

- 1/4 cup plain yogurt
- 2 tablespoons olive oil
- 2 tablespoons lemon juice
- 2 cloves garlic, minced
- 1 teaspoon ground cumin
- 1 teaspoon paprika
- 1/2 teaspoon ground coriander
- 1/2 teaspoon ground cinnamon
- 1/2 teaspoon salt
- 1/4 teaspoon black pepper
- 1/4 teaspoon cayenne pepper (optional, for heat)

For the Kebabs:

- 1 1/2 pounds lamb leg or shoulder, cut into 1-inch cubes
- 1 red onion, cut into chunks
- 1 bell pepper (red, yellow, or green), cut into chunks
- Cherry tomatoes (optional)
- Wooden or metal skewers, soaked in water (if using wooden skewers)

For Serving:

- Chopped fresh parsley or cilantro
- Lemon wedges
- Pita bread or flatbread
- Tzatziki sauce or yogurt sauce

Instructions:

1. Prepare Marinade:
    - In a bowl, combine plain yogurt, olive oil, lemon juice, minced garlic, ground cumin, paprika, ground coriander, ground cinnamon, salt, black pepper, and cayenne pepper (if using). Mix well to combine.

2. Marinate Lamb:
   - Place the cubed lamb in a shallow dish or resealable plastic bag. Pour the marinade over the lamb, making sure it's well coated. Cover the dish or seal the bag, and refrigerate for at least 1 hour, or preferably overnight, to allow the flavors to meld together.
3. Assemble Kebabs:
   - If using wooden skewers, soak them in water for at least 30 minutes to prevent burning on the grill.
   - Preheat your grill to medium-high heat.
   - Thread the marinated lamb cubes onto the skewers, alternating with chunks of red onion and bell pepper. Add cherry tomatoes between the lamb and vegetables if desired.
4. Grill Kebabs:
   - Place the assembled kebabs on the preheated grill. Grill for 8-10 minutes, turning occasionally, or until the lamb is cooked to your desired doneness and the vegetables are tender and slightly charred.
5. Serve:
   - Once cooked, remove the kebabs from the grill and transfer them to a serving platter.
   - Garnish the lamb kebabs with chopped fresh parsley or cilantro. Serve hot with lemon wedges, pita bread or flatbread, and tzatziki sauce or yogurt sauce on the side.
6. Enjoy:
   - Enjoy your homemade lamb kebabs as a delicious and satisfying meal!

Feel free to customize the marinade and kebab ingredients according to your taste preferences. You can also add other vegetables such as mushrooms, zucchini, or eggplant to the kebabs for extra flavor and variety.

Pork Schnitzel

Ingredients:

- 4 boneless pork loin chops, about 1/2 inch thick
- Salt and black pepper to taste
- 1/2 cup all-purpose flour
- 2 large eggs
- 1 cup breadcrumbs (plain or seasoned)
- Vegetable oil, for frying
- Lemon wedges, for serving
- Chopped parsley, for garnish (optional)

Instructions:

1. Prepare Pork Cutlets:
   - Place each pork loin chop between two sheets of plastic wrap or wax paper. Use a meat mallet or rolling pin to pound the pork chops to an even thickness of about 1/4 inch. Season both sides of the pork cutlets with salt and black pepper.
2. Set Up Breading Station:
   - Set up a breading station with three shallow dishes: one with flour, one with beaten eggs, and one with breadcrumbs.
3. Bread Pork Cutlets:
   - Dredge each seasoned pork cutlet first in the flour, shaking off any excess, then in the beaten eggs, and finally in the breadcrumbs, pressing gently to coat evenly. Place the breaded pork cutlets on a baking sheet lined with parchment paper.
4. Heat Oil:
   - In a large skillet, heat enough vegetable oil over medium-high heat to cover the bottom of the skillet. Heat the oil until it shimmers and is hot enough for frying (around 350°F or 175°C).
5. Fry Pork Schnitzel:
   - Carefully add the breaded pork cutlets to the hot oil in a single layer, making sure not to overcrowd the skillet. Depending on the size of your skillet, you may need to fry the schnitzel in batches.
   - Fry the pork schnitzel until golden brown and crispy on both sides, about 3-4 minutes per side. Use tongs to flip the schnitzel halfway through cooking.

- Once cooked, transfer the fried pork schnitzel to a plate lined with paper towels to drain excess oil.
6. Serve:
    - Serve the pork schnitzel hot, garnished with chopped parsley (if desired) and accompanied by lemon wedges for squeezing over the schnitzel.
    - Pork schnitzel pairs well with traditional sides like mashed potatoes, German potato salad, or a fresh salad.
7. Enjoy:
    - Enjoy your homemade pork schnitzel as a delicious and comforting meal!

Pork schnitzel is a versatile dish, and you can customize it by adding spices or herbs to the breadcrumbs or serving it with different sauces or accompaniments.

Shrimp Gumbo

Ingredients:

For the Roux:

- 1/2 cup vegetable oil
- 1/2 cup all-purpose flour

For the Gumbo:

- 1 pound medium shrimp, peeled and deveined
- 1/2 pound Andouille sausage, sliced
- 1 onion, chopped
- 1 bell pepper, chopped
- 2 celery stalks, chopped
- 3 cloves garlic, minced
- 4 cups chicken or seafood broth
- 1 can (14.5 ounces) diced tomatoes
- 1 cup okra, sliced (fresh or frozen)
- 2 bay leaves
- 1 teaspoon dried thyme
- 1 teaspoon paprika
- 1/2 teaspoon cayenne pepper (adjust to taste)
- Salt and black pepper to taste
- Cooked white rice for serving
- Chopped green onions for garnish

Instructions:

1. Make Roux:
    - In a large, heavy-bottomed pot or Dutch oven, heat vegetable oil over medium heat. Gradually whisk in the flour to create a smooth paste. Cook, stirring constantly, for 20-30 minutes or until the roux reaches a dark chocolate color. Be careful not to burn it.
2. Cook Shrimp and Sausage:
    - Once the roux is darkened, add the sliced Andouille sausage to the pot. Cook, stirring occasionally, until the sausage is browned, about 5 minutes.

- Add the peeled and deveined shrimp to the pot. Cook until the shrimp turn pink and are cooked through, about 2-3 minutes. Remove the shrimp and sausage from the pot and set aside.

3. Sauté Aromatics:
   - In the same pot, add chopped onion, bell pepper, celery, and minced garlic. Cook, stirring occasionally, until the vegetables are softened, about 5-7 minutes.
4. Add Broth and Seasonings:
   - Pour in chicken or seafood broth and diced tomatoes with their juices. Add sliced okra, bay leaves, dried thyme, paprika, cayenne pepper, salt, and black pepper to taste. Stir well to combine.
5. Simmer Gumbo:
   - Bring the gumbo to a simmer over medium heat. Reduce the heat to low, cover, and let it simmer gently for 45 minutes to 1 hour, stirring occasionally, until the flavors meld together and the gumbo thickens.
6. Add Shrimp and Sausage:
   - Return the cooked shrimp and sausage to the pot. Stir well to incorporate them into the gumbo. Let the gumbo simmer for an additional 5-10 minutes to heat through.
7. Serve:
   - Once the gumbo is cooked and thickened to your liking, remove the bay leaves.
   - Serve the shrimp gumbo hot over cooked white rice.
   - Garnish each serving with chopped green onions.
8. Enjoy:
   - Enjoy your homemade shrimp gumbo, a flavorful and comforting dish perfect for any occasion!

Feel free to adjust the seasoning and spice level of the gumbo according to your taste preferences. You can also add other ingredients such as crab meat, chicken, or additional vegetables to customize the gumbo to your liking.

Caprese Salad

Ingredients:

- 2 large ripe tomatoes, sliced
- 8 ounces fresh mozzarella cheese, sliced
- Fresh basil leaves
- Extra-virgin olive oil
- Balsamic vinegar (or balsamic glaze)
- Salt and freshly ground black pepper, to taste

Instructions:

1. Slice Tomatoes and Mozzarella:
    - Wash and slice the tomatoes into 1/4-inch thick slices. Similarly, slice the fresh mozzarella cheese into 1/4-inch thick slices as well.
2. Arrange Ingredients:
    - Arrange the tomato and mozzarella slices alternately on a serving platter or individual plates, overlapping them slightly.
3. Add Basil Leaves:
    - Place fresh basil leaves on top of each tomato and mozzarella slice. You can use whole leaves or tear them into smaller pieces.
4. Season:
    - Drizzle extra-virgin olive oil over the tomato and mozzarella slices. Sprinkle with a pinch of salt and freshly ground black pepper to taste.
5. Optional Dressing:
    - For added flavor, you can drizzle balsamic vinegar or balsamic glaze over the Caprese salad just before serving. The tangy sweetness of balsamic vinegar pairs wonderfully with the fresh ingredients.
6. Serve:
    - Serve the Caprese salad immediately as a light and refreshing appetizer or side dish.
7. Enjoy:
    - Enjoy your homemade Caprese salad with its vibrant colors and delicious flavors!

Caprese salad is best enjoyed when made with ripe, seasonal tomatoes and fresh mozzarella cheese. It's a versatile dish that can be served as a starter, a side dish, or even as a light main course. Feel free to customize it by adding ingredients like avocado, olives, or pine nuts, or by drizzling with pesto instead of balsamic vinegar.

Chicken Satay

Ingredients:

For the Chicken Satay:

- 1 pound boneless, skinless chicken breasts or thighs, cut into thin strips
- Wooden skewers, soaked in water for at least 30 minutes (or use metal skewers)

For the Marinade:

- 1/4 cup coconut milk
- 2 tablespoons soy sauce
- 2 tablespoons lime juice
- 2 tablespoons brown sugar
- 2 cloves garlic, minced
- 1 teaspoon ground turmeric
- 1 teaspoon ground coriander
- 1/2 teaspoon ground cumin
- 1/2 teaspoon ground ginger
- 1/4 teaspoon cayenne pepper (optional, for heat)

For the Peanut Sauce:

- 1/2 cup creamy peanut butter
- 1/4 cup coconut milk
- 2 tablespoons soy sauce
- 2 tablespoons lime juice
- 1 tablespoon brown sugar
- 1 clove garlic, minced
- 1 teaspoon ground ginger
- 1/4 teaspoon cayenne pepper (optional, for heat)
- Water (as needed to adjust consistency)

For Serving:

- Chopped peanuts
- Chopped cilantro or parsley
- Lime wedges

Instructions:

1. Prepare Chicken:
   - If using wooden skewers, soak them in water for at least 30 minutes to prevent burning.
   - Cut the chicken breasts or thighs into thin strips, about 1/2 inch wide and 4 inches long.
2. Make Marinade:
   - In a bowl, whisk together the coconut milk, soy sauce, lime juice, brown sugar, minced garlic, ground turmeric, ground coriander, ground cumin, ground ginger, and cayenne pepper (if using) to make the marinade.
3. Marinate Chicken:
   - Place the chicken strips in a shallow dish or resealable plastic bag. Pour the marinade over the chicken, making sure it's well coated. Cover the dish or seal the bag, and refrigerate for at least 30 minutes, or preferably up to 4 hours, to allow the flavors to meld together.
4. Make Peanut Sauce:
   - In a small saucepan over low heat, combine the peanut butter, coconut milk, soy sauce, lime juice, brown sugar, minced garlic, ground ginger, and cayenne pepper (if using) to make the peanut sauce. Cook, stirring constantly, until the peanut butter is melted and the sauce is smooth. If the sauce is too thick, you can thin it out with a little water. Remove from heat and set aside.
5. Skewer Chicken:
   - Preheat your grill or grill pan to medium-high heat. Thread the marinated chicken strips onto the soaked skewers, dividing them evenly among the skewers.
6. Grill Chicken Satay:
   - Grill the chicken skewers for 3-4 minutes per side, or until the chicken is cooked through and slightly charred on the edges.
7. Serve:
   - Serve the grilled chicken satay hot with the peanut sauce on the side.
   - Garnish with chopped peanuts, chopped cilantro or parsley, and lime wedges for squeezing over the chicken.
8. Enjoy:
   - Enjoy your homemade chicken satay with peanut sauce as a delicious appetizer or main course!

Chicken satay is often served with steamed rice, cucumber salad, or Thai-style pickled vegetables for a complete meal. Feel free to adjust the level of spiciness in the marinade and peanut sauce according to your taste preferences.

Beef Teriyaki

Ingredients:

For the Beef:

- 1 pound beef steak (such as sirloin, flank, or ribeye), thinly sliced
- Salt and black pepper, to taste
- 2 tablespoons vegetable oil (for cooking)

For the Teriyaki Sauce:

- 1/2 cup soy sauce
- 1/4 cup mirin (Japanese sweet rice wine)
- 1/4 cup sake (Japanese rice wine) or dry sherry
- 2 tablespoons brown sugar (adjust to taste)
- 2 cloves garlic, minced
- 1 teaspoon grated ginger
- 1 tablespoon cornstarch mixed with 2 tablespoons water (optional, for thickening)

For Serving:

- Cooked white rice
- Steamed vegetables (such as broccoli, carrots, or snow peas)
- Sesame seeds, for garnish (optional)
- Sliced green onions, for garnish (optional)

Instructions:

1. Prepare Beef:
   - If the beef slices are not already thinly sliced, place the beef steak in the freezer for about 20-30 minutes to firm it up, which will make it easier to slice thinly. Once firm, slice the beef against the grain into thin strips. Season the beef strips with salt and black pepper.
2. Make Teriyaki Sauce:
   - In a small saucepan, combine soy sauce, mirin, sake, brown sugar, minced garlic, and grated ginger to make the teriyaki sauce. Bring the mixture to a

simmer over medium heat, stirring occasionally, until the sugar is dissolved and the sauce has slightly thickened, about 5-7 minutes.
- If you prefer a thicker sauce, you can add the cornstarch-water mixture to the sauce and cook for an additional 1-2 minutes until the sauce has thickened to your desired consistency. Remove from heat and set aside.

3. Cook Beef:
   - Heat vegetable oil in a large skillet or wok over medium-high heat. Add the seasoned beef slices to the skillet in a single layer, making sure not to overcrowd the pan. Cook in batches if necessary.
   - Sear the beef slices for 1-2 minutes on each side, or until browned and cooked to your desired doneness. Remove the cooked beef from the skillet and set aside.
4. Glaze with Teriyaki Sauce:
   - Pour the prepared teriyaki sauce into the skillet. Return the cooked beef slices to the skillet and toss to coat evenly in the sauce. Cook for an additional 1-2 minutes, stirring occasionally, until the beef is heated through and glazed with the teriyaki sauce.
5. Serve:
   - Serve the beef teriyaki hot over cooked white rice.
   - Garnish with sesame seeds and sliced green onions, if desired.
   - Serve alongside steamed vegetables for a complete meal.
6. Enjoy:
   - Enjoy your homemade beef teriyaki, with its tender slices of beef coated in a flavorful teriyaki sauce!

Beef teriyaki is a versatile dish that can be served as a main course for dinner or as part of a bento box for lunch. Adjust the sweetness and saltiness of the teriyaki sauce according to your taste preferences.

Spinach Lasagna

Ingredients:

For the Spinach Filling:

- 1 tablespoon olive oil
- 1 onion, chopped
- 3 cloves garlic, minced
- 10 ounces fresh spinach, chopped (or use frozen spinach, thawed and squeezed dry)
- 15 ounces ricotta cheese
- 1/2 cup grated Parmesan cheese
- 1 egg
- Salt and black pepper, to taste
- Pinch of nutmeg (optional)

For the Lasagna:

- 9 lasagna noodles (oven-ready or pre-cooked according to package instructions)
- 2 cups shredded mozzarella cheese
- 1 1/2 cups marinara sauce (homemade or store-bought)

Instructions:

1. Prepare Spinach Filling:
    - In a large skillet, heat olive oil over medium heat. Add chopped onion and minced garlic, and cook until softened, about 5 minutes.
    - Add chopped spinach to the skillet and cook until wilted, about 3-4 minutes. If using frozen spinach, make sure it's thawed and squeezed dry before adding to the skillet.
    - In a bowl, combine cooked spinach mixture with ricotta cheese, grated Parmesan cheese, egg, salt, black pepper, and a pinch of nutmeg if using. Mix until well combined. Set aside.
2. Assemble Lasagna:
    - Preheat your oven to 375°F (190°C).
    - Spread a thin layer of marinara sauce on the bottom of a 9x13-inch baking dish.

- Arrange 3 lasagna noodles over the sauce, covering the bottom of the dish.
- Spread half of the spinach mixture over the noodles, followed by a layer of marinara sauce and shredded mozzarella cheese.
- Repeat the layers: noodles, remaining spinach mixture, marinara sauce, and shredded mozzarella cheese.
- Top with a final layer of noodles, marinara sauce, and shredded mozzarella cheese.

3. Bake Lasagna:
    - Cover the baking dish with aluminum foil and bake in the preheated oven for 30 minutes.
    - Remove the foil and bake for an additional 15 minutes, or until the cheese is bubbly and golden brown.
4. Serve:
    - Let the spinach lasagna cool for a few minutes before slicing and serving.
    - Garnish with additional grated Parmesan cheese and fresh herbs, if desired.
5. Enjoy:
    - Enjoy your homemade spinach lasagna, with its layers of creamy spinach filling and melted cheese!

Feel free to customize this spinach lasagna recipe by adding other ingredients such as sliced mushrooms, roasted red peppers, or sun-dried tomatoes to the filling. You can also use your favorite marinara sauce or homemade tomato sauce for added flavor.

Peking Duck

Ingredients:

For the Duck:

- 1 whole duck (about 5-6 pounds)
- 2 tablespoons maltose (or honey)
- 2 tablespoons soy sauce
- 2 tablespoons rice vinegar
- 1 tablespoon Chinese five-spice powder
- 2 teaspoons salt
- 1 tablespoon Shaoxing wine (optional)

For Serving:

- Mandarin pancakes (store-bought or homemade)
- Hoisin sauce
- Sliced cucumbers
- Sliced scallions (green onions)

Instructions:

1. Prepare the Duck:
    - Rinse the duck inside and out under cold water. Pat dry with paper towels.
    - In a small saucepan, heat maltose (or honey), soy sauce, rice vinegar, Chinese five-spice powder, salt, and Shaoxing wine over low heat, stirring until well combined and the maltose is melted. Let the mixture cool slightly.
2. Marinate the Duck:
    - Use a skewer or fork to prick the skin of the duck all over, being careful not to pierce the meat. This helps the fat to render and the skin to become crispy during roasting.
    - Brush the duck all over, inside and out, with the marinade mixture. Make sure to coat the duck evenly. Let the duck marinate in the refrigerator for at least 2 hours, or overnight for best results.
3. Roast the Duck:
    - Preheat your oven to 375°F (190°C).

- Place the marinated duck on a wire rack set over a baking sheet to catch any drippings. Roast the duck in the preheated oven for about 2 hours, or until the skin is crispy and golden brown and the internal temperature reaches 165°F (74°C).
- If the skin is getting too dark before the duck is fully cooked, you can tent it loosely with aluminum foil.

4. Serve the Peking Duck:
    - Once the duck is cooked, let it rest for a few minutes before carving.
    - To serve, shred the crispy skin and meat of the duck using a sharp knife or cleaver.
    - Spread hoisin sauce on Mandarin pancakes, top with shredded duck, sliced cucumbers, and sliced scallions. Roll up the pancakes and enjoy!
5. Enjoy:
    - Enjoy your homemade Peking duck with its crispy skin and flavorful meat, served with Mandarin pancakes and your favorite condiments!

While this recipe provides a simplified version of Peking duck that can be made at home without special equipment, traditional Peking duck is often prepared using a more complex method involving air-drying, blanching, and roasting in a wood-fired oven. Adjust the seasonings and ingredients according to your taste preferences.

Pork Carnitas

Ingredients:

- 3-4 pounds pork shoulder (also known as pork butt), trimmed of excess fat and cut into 2-inch chunks
- 1 onion, roughly chopped
- 4 cloves garlic, minced
- 1 orange, juiced
- 2 limes, juiced
- 1 teaspoon ground cumin
- 1 teaspoon dried oregano
- 1 teaspoon smoked paprika
- 1 teaspoon chili powder
- 1 bay leaf
- Salt and black pepper, to taste
- 2 tablespoons vegetable oil

Instructions:

1. Marinate the Pork:
    - In a large bowl or resealable plastic bag, combine the pork chunks, chopped onion, minced garlic, orange juice, lime juice, ground cumin, dried oregano, smoked paprika, chili powder, bay leaf, salt, and black pepper. Mix well to coat the pork evenly. Marinate the pork in the refrigerator for at least 2 hours, or preferably overnight, to allow the flavors to meld together.
2. Cook the Pork:
    - Preheat your oven to 325°F (160°C).
    - Heat vegetable oil in a large Dutch oven or heavy-bottomed pot over medium-high heat. Once hot, add the marinated pork chunks in batches, making sure not to overcrowd the pot. Sear the pork on all sides until browned, about 3-4 minutes per batch. Transfer the seared pork to a plate and set aside.
3. Braise the Pork:
    - Once all the pork chunks are seared, return them to the pot along with any accumulated juices. Add enough water to cover the pork by about 1 inch.
    - Bring the liquid to a simmer, then cover the pot and transfer it to the preheated oven.

- Braise the pork in the oven for 2-3 hours, or until the pork is very tender and easily shreds with a fork.
4. Crisp the Pork:
    - Once the pork is tender, remove the pot from the oven and increase the oven temperature to broil.
    - Use a slotted spoon to transfer the pork chunks to a baking sheet lined with aluminum foil or a wire rack set over a baking sheet.
    - Place the pork under the broiler for 5-10 minutes, or until the edges are crispy and caramelized, turning the pork pieces halfway through to ensure even crisping.
5. Serve:
    - Once the pork carnitas are crispy and golden brown, remove them from the oven.
    - Serve the pork carnitas hot, with your choice of accompaniments such as tortillas, salsa, guacamole, chopped onions, cilantro, lime wedges, or pickled vegetables.
6. Enjoy:
    - Enjoy your homemade pork carnitas as a flavorful and satisfying meal!

Feel free to customize your pork carnitas by adjusting the seasonings or adding additional spices according to your taste preferences. You can also use the cooked pork carnitas as a filling for tacos, burritos, quesadillas, or salads.

Moussaka

Ingredients:

For the Meat Sauce:

- 1 pound ground lamb or beef
- 1 onion, finely chopped
- 3 cloves garlic, minced
- 1 can (14.5 ounces) diced tomatoes
- 2 tablespoons tomato paste
- 1 teaspoon dried oregano
- 1 teaspoon dried thyme
- 1/2 teaspoon ground cinnamon
- Salt and black pepper, to taste
- Olive oil, for cooking

For the Eggplant and Potatoes:

- 2 large eggplants, sliced into 1/2-inch rounds
- 2 large potatoes, peeled and sliced into 1/4-inch rounds
- Olive oil, for brushing
- Salt and black pepper, to taste

For the Béchamel Sauce:

- 4 tablespoons unsalted butter
- 1/4 cup all-purpose flour
- 2 cups milk
- Pinch of nutmeg
- Salt and black pepper, to taste
- 1/2 cup grated Parmesan cheese
- 2 large eggs, beaten

Instructions:

1. Prepare the Eggplant and Potatoes:
    - Preheat your oven to 400°F (200°C).

- Arrange the sliced eggplant and potato rounds on baking sheets lined with parchment paper.
- Brush the eggplant and potato slices with olive oil on both sides. Season with salt and black pepper.
- Roast in the preheated oven for 20-25 minutes, or until tender and lightly browned. Remove from the oven and set aside.

2. Prepare the Meat Sauce:
   - In a large skillet or saucepan, heat a drizzle of olive oil over medium heat. Add the chopped onion and minced garlic, and sauté until softened.
   - Add the ground lamb or beef to the skillet, breaking it up with a spoon. Cook until browned.
   - Stir in the diced tomatoes, tomato paste, dried oregano, dried thyme, ground cinnamon, salt, and black pepper. Simmer the sauce for about 15-20 minutes, until thickened. Remove from heat and set aside.

3. Prepare the Béchamel Sauce:
   - In a medium saucepan, melt the butter over medium heat. Once melted, whisk in the flour to create a roux. Cook the roux for 1-2 minutes, stirring constantly.
   - Gradually whisk in the milk, a little at a time, until smooth and thickened. Cook the sauce for a few minutes until it reaches a creamy consistency.
   - Season the béchamel sauce with a pinch of nutmeg, salt, and black pepper. Remove from heat and let it cool slightly.
   - Stir in the grated Parmesan cheese and beaten eggs until well combined. Set aside.

4. Assemble the Moussaka:
   - Grease a 9x13-inch baking dish with olive oil. Arrange half of the roasted eggplant slices in the bottom of the dish, overlapping slightly.
   - Top the eggplant with half of the meat sauce, spreading it evenly.
   - Layer the sliced potatoes on top of the meat sauce, followed by the remaining eggplant slices.
   - Pour the remaining meat sauce over the eggplant layer, spreading it out evenly.

5. Finish Assembling:
   - Pour the prepared béchamel sauce over the top of the meat sauce layer, spreading it out with a spatula to cover the entire surface.

6. Bake the Moussaka:
   - Place the assembled moussaka in the preheated oven and bake for 45-50 minutes, or until the top is golden brown and bubbly.

7. Serve:

- Remove the moussaka from the oven and let it cool for a few minutes before slicing.
- Serve the moussaka warm, garnished with chopped fresh herbs if desired.

8. Enjoy:
    - Enjoy your homemade moussaka, a hearty and flavorful Mediterranean dish!

Moussaka is traditionally served warm or at room temperature and pairs well with a simple salad or crusty bread. Feel free to customize the recipe by adding other vegetables or herbs to the meat sauce or adjusting the seasoning to suit your taste preferences.

Beef Pho

Ingredients:

For the Broth:

- 4 pounds beef bones (such as oxtail, knuckle bones, or marrow bones)
- 1 onion, halved
- 1 knob of ginger (about 3 inches), sliced
- 5 star anise pods
- 4 whole cloves
- 2 cinnamon sticks
- 1 cardamom pod
- 1 tablespoon coriander seeds
- 1 tablespoon salt
- 1 tablespoon sugar
- Water, enough to cover the bones (about 4-5 quarts)
- Fish sauce, to taste (optional)

For the Soup:

- 12 ounces dried rice noodles (banh pho)
- 1 pound beef sirloin or flank steak, thinly sliced
- Garnishes: fresh bean sprouts, Thai basil leaves, cilantro, thinly sliced onions, lime wedges, thinly sliced chili peppers

Instructions:

1. Prepare the Broth:
    - Place the beef bones in a large stockpot and cover with cold water. Bring to a boil over high heat, then reduce the heat to low and simmer for 10 minutes. Drain the bones and rinse under cold water to remove any impurities.
    - Return the bones to the pot and cover with fresh water. Add the halved onion and sliced ginger.
    - Toast the star anise, cloves, cinnamon sticks, cardamom pod, and coriander seeds in a dry skillet over medium heat until fragrant, about 1-2 minutes. Add the toasted spices to the pot.

- Add salt and sugar to the pot and bring the broth to a gentle simmer. Skim off any foam that rises to the surface.
- Simmer the broth, uncovered, for at least 4 hours, or preferably 6-8 hours, to extract maximum flavor from the bones. Add more water if needed to keep the bones covered.
- Strain the broth through a fine-mesh sieve or cheesecloth into a clean pot. Discard the solids. Taste the broth and adjust seasoning with fish sauce if desired.

2. Prepare the Noodles and Beef:
   - Cook the dried rice noodles according to the package instructions. Drain and rinse under cold water to stop the cooking process. Set aside.
   - Thinly slice the beef sirloin or flank steak against the grain. Set aside.

3. Assemble the Beef Pho:
   - Divide the cooked rice noodles among serving bowls. Top with thinly sliced raw beef.
   - Ladle hot broth over the noodles and beef, ensuring that the beef is fully submerged in the hot broth. The heat of the broth will cook the beef slices.
   - Serve the beef pho hot, accompanied by a platter of fresh bean sprouts, Thai basil leaves, cilantro, thinly sliced onions, lime wedges, and thinly sliced chili peppers. Diners can add these garnishes to their bowls according to their taste preferences.

4. Enjoy:
   - Enjoy your homemade beef pho, a comforting and aromatic noodle soup that's perfect for any occasion!

Beef pho is a versatile dish, and you can customize it by adding other ingredients such as beef tendon, brisket, or meatballs. Adjust the seasoning of the broth to your taste preferences by adding more salt, sugar, or fish sauce as needed.

www.ingramcontent.com/pod-product-compliance
Lightning Source LLC
LaVergne TN
LVHW061940070526
838199LV00060B/3888